VICTORIA & ABDUL

Shrabani Basu is a journalist and author. Her books include *For King and Another Country, Indian Soldiers on the Western Front 1914–18, Victoria & Abdul, The True Story of the Queen's Closest Confidant, Spy Princess, The Life of Noor Inayat Khan* and *Curry: the Story of Britain's Favourite Dish*. She has edited *Reimagine: India–UK Cultural Relations in the Twenty-First Century*. She writes regularly for the Indian newspapers *ABP* and the *Telegraph* and has contributed to the *Daily Express, Mail on Sunday* and other publications. She is founder and chair of the Noor Inayat Khan Memorial Trust.

Lee Hall was born in Newcastle in 1966. He started writing for radio in 1995, winning awards for *I Luv You Jimmy Spud, Spoonface Steinberg* and *Blood Sugar*, all of which made the journey to other media. His screenplay for *Billy Elliot* was nominated for an Oscar and was adapted into the multi-award-winning stage musical. *The Pitmen Painters* received the *Evening Standard* Best Play Award and TMA Best New Play Award. *Our Ladies of Perpetual Succour* premiered at the Traverse Theatre, Edinburgh, in 2015 and transferred to the National Theatre, London, the following year. The play won the Olivier Award for Best New Comedy and transferred to the Duke of York's, London, in 2017. He has worked as writer-in-residence for Live Theatre, Newcastle, and the Royal Shakespeare Company, and has adapted many plays for the stage, including Goldoni's *A Servant to Two Masters* (Young Vic/RSC), Brecht's *Mr Puntila and His Man Matti* (Right Size/Almeida) and Heijermans' *The Good Hope* (National).

also by Lee Hall from Faber

BILLY ELLIOT: THE SCREENPLAY
THE PITMEN PAINTERS
OUR LADIES OF PERPETUAL SUCCOUR
SHAKESPEARE IN LOVE
(*based on the screenplay by Marc Norman and Tom Stoppard*)

published by BBC Books

SPOONFACE STEINBERG AND OTHER PLAYS

published by Methuen

PLAYS: ONE
PLAYS: TWO
THE ADVENTURES OF PINOCCHIO
COOKING WITH ELVIS & BOLLOCKS
THE GOOD HOPE
A SERVANT TO TWO MASTERS

VICTORIA & ABDUL

Lee Hall

Based on the book
VICTORIA & ABDUL: THE TRUE STORY
OF THE QUEEN'S CLOSEST CONFIDANT
by Shrabani Basu

ff

FABER & FABER

First published in 2017
by Faber & Faber Limited
Bloomsbury House
74–77 Great Russell Street
London WC1B 3DA

Typeset by Country Setting, Kingsdown, Kent CT14 8ES
Printed and bound in the UK by CPI Group (UK) Ltd, Croydon CR0 4YY

A CIP record for this book is available from the British Library

ISBN 978-0-571-34222-8

2 4 6 8 10 9 7 5 3 1

INTRODUCTION

Driving down the Holloway Road in London mindlessly listening to someone on the radio talking about curry, I was jolted out of my reverie when I thought I heard them say that the first person to cook a curry for Queen Victoria, Empress of India, was an Indian Muslim manservant who was also not only her most intimate confidant but her spiritual advisor. Could I have heard this correctly? An Indian Muslim manservant who had been a common scrivener in an Agra gaol had become the mentor of the most powerful person on Earth, teaching her Urdu and the Koran? How was this possible? How come I'd not heard of it before?

I leapt out of the car and listened to the whole thing again on iPlayer, not quite believing my ears. I rather incredulously told the story to my wife, the film-maker Beeban Kidron, and a couple of days later we were sitting with Shrabani Basu, the person I'd heard on the radio, who had just finished writing a book about it all.

Shrabani had been researching the history of curry when she came across the story of Abdul's relationship with Queen Victoria. When the Queen died, Abdul became persona non grata and was exiled from Britain. All documentary evidence of his relationship with the Queen was burned, including her thousands of letters to him. But following the story back to Agra where the unfortunate Abdul was finally forced to retreat, Shrabani discovered a number of his private journals, which he'd smuggled out of Britain. Her discovery of Abdul's own writings, long thought to have been lost, gave unprecedented access to the story.

Beeban persuaded Shrabani to entrust the resulting book to us, and I went off to write a script.

The story is rich in so many ways: the outsider who upsets the order of things, the dying monarch, the dying Empire. But what amazed me most was that Victoria herself stood up against the profound racism and condescension of the household and her family, and championed not only the man but his religious beliefs. The fear of Islam that blights us now was no different then, and I quickly recognised this was a story as pertinent today as it ever had been.

To be frank, as a convinced republican I knew very little about Victoria, but the more I found out the more fascinated I became. The ironies and absurdities were just so delicious. The fact that the Queen was made Empress of India after the Mutiny yet could never visit because she'd be assassinated astonished me. The descriptions of the gargantuan meals she was expected to consume were equally amazing. Almost everybody who came into close contact with her wrote a memoir at some point and reports of her indecorous table manners made me laugh out loud. I realised the whole thing was grand comedy.

Abdul was pilloried in almost all contemporary commentaries for being some kind of usurper: a self-interested Svengali out to dupe the Queen. But it was clear to me that the Queen was no fool and the story becomes much more interesting when you take Abdul as seriously as Victoria did. Far from being an Indian Tartuffe, Abdul seemed more like an innocent abroad. If anything he was an 'Uncle Tom' who received rather rough justice for misjudging the institutional racism and malevolence at the core of the Empire.

Yet at the heart of it all is a love story between an eighty-year-old woman who happened to be the richest and most powerful person on earth and a young Indian nobody. It seemed to speak about all the contradictions of power. When one examined it carefully it became less and less clear who was the master and who the slave. Ultimately India gained independence and, certainly in my version of events, the Queen receives some liberatory trans-cendence because of Abdul's good offices. So although this is in part a sad tale of racism and an indictment of empire it is also, potentially, a hopeful one where simple kindness and love can disrupt some of that manifest iniquity.

Beeban introduced me to Stephen Frears, whose beady eye for the preposterousness of any convention and his generally wicked sense of irony was a perfect match for my 'subaltern' take on the pretensions of empire. He immediately announced that the film was impossible to make without Judi Dench, which rather put the kibosh on everything as Judi had already played Queen Vic and is famously disinclined to revisit old roles. Undeterred Stephen went off to visit Judi and came back with the news that she'd read the script and was officially on board.

Judi is every writer's dream. Her wit, warmth, humour, absolute skill and perfect taste were simply thrilling to watch every day. Then to see Ali Fazal rise to meet the formidable challenge of matching her was a wonderful thing. Indeed, Stephen put together an astonishing cast of actors who seemed to perfectly understand that although this was a comedy it must be played with an emotional truth, and so, of course, it was all the funnier.

Inevitably a final film is never the same as the initial screenplay. Certain things work on the page but less so when they are fully inhabited. Our boredom threshold reduces when we watch things rather than read them, a look can say as much as a whole scene, the order of events can sit better back to front . . . But in this case the film is not so very different from the screenplay. Largely what I'd written is what's up there, so I decided to publish the script we took into the shoot rather than a simple transcription of the movie. What always interests me are the details that were shot but didn't make it into the final cut, the storylines that had to be trimmed, the little revelations which add substance or depth to a character. So here it is – warts and all.

There are too many people to thank individually but I have to doff my cap to Stephen Frears who really stuck by the story, Shrabani Basu who entrusted us with her very precious book, Tracey Seward and Melanie Oliver without whom we'd have been nowhere, and Eric Felner, my friend and long-term collaborator, who made the whole thing happen.

But I'd like to dedicate this book to Beeban who saw the script and film through every single step of its journey. And to the memory of Tim Pigott-Smith. I delighted every day in his brilliance on set and his immense kindness off it. A truly lovely and remarkable human being.

LH, August 2017

MAIN CAST AND CREW

Focus Features and BBC Films present
in association with Perfect World Pictures
a Working Title production
in association with Cross Street Films
A Stephen Frears Film

QUEEN VICTORIA	Judi Dench
LORD SALISBURY	Michael Gambon
BARONESS CHURCHILL	Olivier Williams
BERTIE, PRINCE OF WALES	Eddie Izzard
MR PUCCINI	Simon Callow
MOHAMMED	Adeel Akhtar
SIR HENRY PONSONBY	Tim Piggot-Smith
ALICK YORKE	Julian Wadham
ABDUL KARIM	Ali Fazal
MISS PHIPPS	Fenella Woolgar
PAGE BOY	Benjamin Haigh
QUEEN'S FOOTMAN	Lasco Atkins
MRS TUCK	Ruth McCabe
KAISER WILHELM II	Jonathan Harden
ARTHUR BIGGE	Robin Soans

Music by	Thomas Newman
Make-Up and Hair Designer	Daniel Phillips
Costume Designer	Consolata Boyle
Editor	Melanie Ann Oliver, Ace Production
Designer	Alan Macdonald
Director of Photography	Danny Cohen, Bsc
Executive Producers	Lee Hall, Amelia Granger. Liza Chasin, Christine Langan Joe Oppenheimer
Based on the book by	Shrabani Basu
Screenplay by	Lee Hall
Produced by	Tim Bevan, Eric Fellner, Beeban Kidron. Tracey Seaward
Directed by	Stephen Frears

Victoria & Abdul

Dialogue in bold is in Hindi with English subtitles.

Words appear on screen:

AGRA, 1886
BRITAIN HAS FORMALLY RULED INDIA
FOR TWENTY-EIGHT YEARS

INT. ABDUL'S ROOM, INDIA

A darkened room. Someone is moving in the darkness. Then the shutters of the room are thrown wide open and the blinding light reveals: Abdul, twenty-four, smiling into the sun – we hear sound of the muezzin's call to prayer in the distance.

EXT. ROOF TOP, AGRA

Abdul praying in the glorious sunshine. We see all of Agra below him, the Taj Mahal in the distance.

EXT. STREET, AGRA

Abdul rushes out of a squalid doorway into the bustle of the street. As he hurries through the jammed streets he acknowledges people as he goes, making his way past the lame and sick, through crowds, spice stalls. Suddenly he accidentally bumps into a white colonial officer:

OFFICER

Idiot!

The officer has already turned away so Abdul hurries on through the dusty streets.

EXT. AGRA GAOL. THE SAME

Donkeys, a dog pisses on the wall. Abdul hurries in.

INT. AGRA GAOL

Abdul bows to the guard enthusiastically. The lugubrious guard unlocks several locks on the rusting iron gate. The door slams shut.

Abdul hurries along the corridor. We see pitiful inmates, all at looms making carpets, watched by bored, unshaven guards.

Abdul rushes to his high desk and starts on the Sisyphean task of compiling the prison ledgers with huge concentration. Abdul looks up to see the prison guard.

GUARD

Tyler wants to see you. Now.

INT. TYLER'S OFFICE. THE SAME

A faded, mildewed monochrome of a young Queen Victoria on the wall. Abdul is underneath looking nervously at Tyler, the Prison Governor.

TYLER

Ah, Mr Karim. I wanted to speak to you about the carpets we sent to the Exhibition.

ABDUL

There is problem, sir?

TYLER

No. No. The carpets went down very well. In fact the Governor General has received a letter from the Royal Household thanking him personally. The whole thing's been such a success he has decided to present the Queen with a mohar as part of the Jubilee.

ABDUL

A mohar, sir?

TYLER

A mohar. Apparently it's a sort of ceremonial coin, rather like a medal. I have been asked to find someone tall to present it. Well, you're the tallest person here.

ABDUL

Mr Tyler! When will she be arriving, sir?

TYLER

Not in Agra. In England.

ABDUL

England?!

TYLER

You'll present the mohar at an official function. Like an equerry.

ABDUL

On a horse?

TYLER

I don't think there'll be a horse.

ABDUL

An equerry always has a horse, Mr Tyler, sir.

TYLER

Well, maybe not like an equerry exactly. They were actually after Hindus but I thought you'd do. What do you say?

ABDUL

Are you sure there isn't a horse?

INT. QUEEN'S BEDROOM. ENGLAND

Another dark room. The curtains are thrown, light streams into the room. We see Mrs Tuck at the window. In the shadows is a large bed into which a enormous mound appears to be upholstered.

MRS TUCK

Good morning, Your Majesty.

We cut to:

EXT. ENTRANCE TO DOCKS

Abdul is now with Tyler, a portly Englishman, Bigge, and what looks like his short, squat Indian manservant.

TYLER

This is Mr Bigge – extra Groom in Waiting to the Royal Household who will be in charge. This is Abdul.

7

                    BIGGE
This is Mohammed.

                    TYLER
He's very short.

                    BIGGE
We had to swop him at the last minute. The tall guy had an
accident with an elephant.

Abdul beams at Mohammed, who is distinctly unhappy.

                    ABDUL
Hi!

Mohammed looks sourly and does not respond.

INT. QUEEN'S BEDCHAMBER

*A group of straining footmen roll Queen Victoria over and then
manhandle her out of bed.*

EXT. ON DECK AT SEA. DAY

*Abdul and Mohammed standing in front of Bigge, who has a chart on
a tripod.*

                    BIGGE
At the top there's the Private Secretary, then there are the
Ladies in Waiting, the Upper Servants, the lower Upper
Servants, the members of the Household, the Head of the
Household staff – splitting into three parts: the head of the
Bedchamber, the personal head of staff, the Butler in
Chief, who is in charge of the Household Butler, the
kitchen factotum, head of kitchen, the head of waiting staff,
the ordinary waiting staff (Windsor), the table maids, then
you. Any questions?

                    ABDUL
Who will have the mohar, sir?

                    BIGGE
I'm not exactly sure, as yet. I suspect you will both carry it.
On a cushion.

ABDUL

We both have a cushion?

BIGGE

No, there'll only be one cushion. Between you.

ABDUL

Can we have a cushion now, sir?

BIGGE

You'll have to mime the cushion.

ABDUL

I don't understand, sir.

BIGGE

Pretend. You'll have to pretend the cushion is there. Like this. The key to good service is standing still and moving backward. The most important thing is you must not look at her.

ABDUL

But how will we present the mohar, sir?!

BIGGE

You put out the cushion and avert your gaze, appropriately. Her Majesty will take the mohar and you will egress retrospectively in a stately manner.

MOHAMMED

What an arsehole.

INT. OUTSIDE THE QUEEN'S BEDCHAMBER

A line of dressers, ladies-in-waiting, footmen, equerries etc. all parade into the Queen's bedchamber.

INT. CABIN. AT SEA

Abdul and Mohammed in their tiny cell. Mohammed has a pile of buns. He passes one to Abdul.

MOHAMMED

Have you any idea how cold it is? We're gonna bloody
die there.

ABDUL

Why on earth did you agree to come?

MOHAMMED

Had no choice. The tall guy fell off an elephant and I got
drafted in at the last moment. Five thousand miles to
present a bloody medal.

ABDUL

But it's a very great honour.

MOHAMMED

Honour?! My father fought in the Mutiny. Have you
tasted English food? They eat pig's blood.

ABDUL

They do not eat pig's blood!

MOHAMMED

I'm telling you they have pig's blood in sausages. And
the brains of sheep. The place is barbaric.

ABDUL

Not to worry.

Abdul shows Mohammed a little tin containing a load of spices.

A present from my mother.

MOHAMMED

My advice: eat as much as you can before we hit land.

He passes Abdul another bun.

Let's give her the medal and get the hell back home.

TILBURY DOCKS. DAY

*The huge exodus. Abdul, Mohammed come down the gangplank with
Arthur Bigge.*

BIGGE

Civilisation!

The posh English people buffet Abdul and Mohammed in the mad rush to the quayside. Finally, they look at the hawkers, scrawny porters, the distinctly uncivilised detritus of Victorian London. A beggar holds out his hand to Abdul.

BEGGAR

Give uz a farthing.

INT. QUEEN'S BEDCHAMBER. THE SAME

The Queen is sitting on a stool with her back to us. A gaggle of dressers stand with the Queen's garments.

MRS TUCK

Arms.

The Queen puts her arms up.

INT. GENTLEMAN TAILOR'S, LONDON. DAY

Wood-panelled room. Men in suits. Abdul and Mohammed are dressed in strange Indian costumes.

TAILOR

Arms.

Abdul puts his arms up as the tailor fixes a sash around him.

BIGGE

Splendid.

TAILOR

We copied them from some drawings in the British Museum.

ABDUL

A sash is not traditional, sir.

TAILOR
(*to Bigge*)
The Indian drawings didn't seem very Indian – so we made some innovations. We need it to look authentic.

BIGGE

It looks jolly good to me.

INT. THE QUEEN'S BEDCHAMBER

A cloud of powder as Mrs Tuck applies a vast powder brush to the Queen. Just as she is about to emerge from the cloud we cut to Ponsonby, Keeper of the Privy Purse and Private Secretary to the Sovereign, reading the day's itinerary.

PONSONBY

Nine o'clock: breakfast in London. Quarter to ten: Trooping of the Colour. Eleven o'clock: elevenses with the Crown Prince Alexander of Norway, the Norwegian Ambassador, the Chief Under-Secretary of State for the Southern Norwegian Provinces and the Junior Under-Secretary . . .

EXT. COURTYARD, WINDSOR CASTLE. DAY

A carriage rushes into the courtyard. Abdul, Mohammed and Arthur Bigge alight. Abdul and Mohammed look in amazement at their surroundings. Over which we hear Ponsonby continuing his speech:

PONSONBY
(*voice-over*)

Midday: luncheon at Buckingham Palace. Two o'clock: ceremonial drive down the Mall . . .

INT. THE SAME, QUEEN'S BEDCHAMBER

Mrs Tuck places the Queen's bonnet on. We still haven't seen her face.

PONSONBY
(*voice-over*)

Two thirty: tea party for thirty thousand children at Hyde Park . . .

INT. THE SAME, CORRIDOR, WINDSOR CASTLE

Bigge, Mohammed and Abdul with their suitcases walking down a corridor in full ceremonial garb.

PONSONBY
(*voice-over*)
Four thirty: royal train to Windsor. Six thirty: full supper. Including the ceremonial presentation of a mohar.

INT. STATE ROOM, WINDSOR CASTLE. DAY

Abdul, Mohammed and Bigge arrive in a vast hall. Tables are laid for an enormous dinner. A crowd of secretaries, officials, waiting staff and other servants are being instructed by Alick Yorke, the portly Director of Ceremonies. He stops mid-sentence. Everybody looks at Abdul and Mohammed in amazement.

BIGGE
The Hindoos, sir.

ALICK YORKE
But they are completely different sizes.

BIGGE
There was an incident with an elephant.

ALICK YORKE
But what on earth are they wearing?

BIGGE
It's ceremonial, sir.

ALICK YORKE
On arrival Her Majesty will process to the main doors. Fanfares. Ceremonial entrance. The Royal Entourage will sit: Her Majesty; the Viceroy of India; the Prince of Wales; Princess Beatrice; Sir Henry Ponsonby, Private Secretary; Lord Salisbury, the Prime Minister; Princess Louise; the Emperor of Russia; Lady Churchill; Lady Mallet; etcetera, etcetera. Grace. Soup: consommé à la Portugaise with purée de madeleine. Fish course: morue à huîtres. Fanfare. Entrées: quenelles with Regency sauce, ballotines de canard

13

with a Cumberland gravy, braised beef à la Hussarde, leg of lamb, the pheasant and those potato ribbon things. Dessert: pain d'épinards, profiteroles au chocolat and tartelettes à la Suisse. The dessert is cleared. Speeches. A fanfare. You –

He grabs Abdul.

ALICK YORKE
– will come from the north-west entrance. Process together. You –

He grabs Mohammed.

ALICK YORKE
– will come to here, and you will stand here – no, a little bit . . . that's it. Presenting the tray thus – the Viceroy will indicate to Her Majesty . . .

ABDUL
Tray?

Everything stops.

ABDUL
I thought it was a cushion.

ALICK YORKE
Who said anything about a cushion? You will present the tray . . .

MOHAMMED
What will I do?

ALICK YORKE
You will stand perfectly still and move backward when required. Her Majesty takes the mohar. What is a mohar?

AN ASSISTANT
It's a coin, sir. Issued by the Moghul Empire.

ALICK YORKE
Why are we presenting it here?! Whatever you do you must not look at Her Majesty. You will bow again. Then moving backwards you will turn to your left – you will lead – thus – and you will process down the hall to be met by Mr Bates

14

who will walk you back to the north wall where you will
stand till the end of the meal. Would you like me to run
through that again?

A page rushes in.

PAGE

Mr Yorke. She's leaving Paddington!

ALICK YORKE

Everybody out.

EXT. COUNTRYSIDE. DAY

The Queen's train. Children wave flags as it passes.

INT. ANTECHAMBER. THE SAME

Hundreds of guests are milling.

INT. KITCHENS, WINDSOR CASTLE

CHEF

Where are the bloody quenelles? You two. Out of it!

*Abdul and Mohammed are evicted from the kitchen by the chef. Then
a voice:*

VOICE

She's at the station!

CHEF

Jesus Christ! SHE'S AT THE STATION!

Abdul and Mohammed are grabbed by Alick Yorke.

ALICK YORKE

For God's sake just wait where you were told. Open the
doors!

INT. LONG CORRIDOR. DAY

A little pageboy runs in shouting:

                    LITTLE PAGEBOY
Open the doors! Open the doors! Open the doors!

INT. THE HALL

*Ushers let the waiting guests into the main hall, all agog with
anticipation.*

INT. SIDE CORRIDOR. THE SAME

*Abdul and Mohammed stand with a huge line of waiters all ready to
start the service.*

EXT. GATE, WINDSOR CASTLE

Carriages sweep past.

INT. THE SAME, CORRIDOR

A pageboy runs at full pelt.

                        PAGEBOY
She's coming! She's coming!

INT. THE SAME, HALL

        The guests are by their chairs. A fanfare.

INT. THE SAME, SIDE CORRIDOR

*Abdul and Mohammad peering out behind Alick Yorke, who looks at
his pocket watch and shouts:*

                    ALICK YORKE

        The soup!

INT. THE SAME, CORRIDOR

The pageboy running.

> PAGEBOY

Soup! Soup!

INT. KITCHENS

> CHEF

Soup!

INT. THE HALL

A fanfare. The main doors fly open. The fanfare reaches its climax.
Enter the Queen. We see her properly for the very first time. She is a
tiny, almost spherical figure, old, frail, glum and dreadfully tired.
Ponsonby leads her to her seat. The entourage follow: the Prince of
Wales, laughing coarsely with Lady Churchill, Dr Reid, various
dignitaries. All completely casual. Everyone else in the hall is frigidly
agog, craning to see the little old lady at the centre. She sits, then utters
an audible sigh of relief. Her bowl of soup is placed in front of her.
She attacks it greedily making a disgusting slurping noise as she eats.
everybody starts to eat.

INT. CORRIDOR. THE SAME

Abdul and Mohammed try to have a gander but are pushed out of the
way by Alick Yorke.

INT. HALL. THE SAME

The Queen has soup all around her mouth and is scraping the bowl to
get the last bit. Then she is finished in record time. She plonks her
spoon on the bowl and cleans her chin with the napkin. Quick as a
flash a waiter removes the bowl. Further down the table, as guests are
amiably enjoying the conversation around them, suddenly waiters
snatch the bowls – still full of soup. Dr Reid addresses a startled diner:

DR REID
I'm afraid you have to be quick. They take it off you as
soon as she's done.

INT. THE SAME, CORRIDOR

*Scores and scores of waiters rush past Abdul and Mohammed carrying
soup bowls.*

ALICK YORKE

One down. Six to go.

Bigge appears with the mohar on a tray.

BIGGE

I have the mohar.

ALICK YORKE

Is that it?!

HEAD WAITER

Sir, the fish course.

ALICK YORKE
(*shouting instructions*)

The fish course!

INT. HALL

*The babble of excited chatter. Everyone around the Queen is
animated. The Queen ignores it all and is shovelling quenelles into her
mouth. Cut to her polishing off the boeuf braisé, then tearing apart a
pheasant.*

*We see Lady Churchill laughing. Lady Phipps, a skinny, terrified-
looking Lady in Waiting is eating salad primly. Back to the Queen:
her plate is clean and she is nodding off.*

PONSONBY

Profiteroles, Your Majesty.

A profiterole is presented and the Queen immediately comes to life.

INT. THE SAME, CORRIDOR

Abdul waits anxiously as streams of waiters bring back the plates from dessert.

ALICK YORKE

The profiteroles have gone. Gentlemen . . .

Alick Yorke makes a final adjustment to the mohar.

ALICK YORKE

Now. Process. Turn. Bow. Present. And absolutely no sodding eye contact what-so-ever!

Abdul takes a huge breath, looks nervously at Mohammed. A trumpet sounds and they walk up the hall. Everybody turns to see the two Indians process with the mohar. The Queen is now talking to the Viceroy and is taking no notice at all of the ceremony. Abdul and Mohammed can see her from the corner of their eye. They reach the head of the table and stop. They turn. Bow. The Queen is still talking and pays them no attention. Ponsonby explains:

PONSONBY

A gift from the Colony of India. A mohar, Your Majesty.

The Queen turns and looks at the mohar, incredulous.

PONSONBY

A coin from the Mughal Empire. In honour of your service to the sub-continent.

Abdul presents the tray bowing his head low. The Queen takes the coin, utterly bemused. Another servant puts a cushion on the table for it to rest on. Abdul doesn't quite know what to do. Ponsonby angrily indicates for them to leave. Abdul takes the hint. They back away as trained.

QUEEN VICTORIA

Are we done?

PONSONBY

We still have coffee, Your Majesty.

Queen Victoria raises her eyes to heaven. Then suddenly looks across at Abdul. He stops, frozen. He smiles at her. She looks at him. The title appears on screen:

VICTORIA AND ABDUL

We hear Mr Bigge sharply chide Abdul.

BIGGE

Eyes!

His smile falls and he drops his head.

INT. DARKENED ROOM. THE FOLLOWING DAY, MORNING

As before: a dark room, a curtain is drawn by Mrs Tuck. The room fills with sunlight and we see we are in the Queen's bedchamber.

MRS TUCK

Good morning, Your Majesty.

Again we see the Queen seemingly upholstered into her bed. The group of servants approach to extract her.

INT. ĐRESSING ROOM. THE SAME

Regal music. The Queen immobile in the centre of the room, as before.

MRS TUCK

Arms.

The Queen lifts her arms. This time we witness the whole unedifying affair. The dresser arrives with a dress and has some trouble getting it over her head. Finally her head is prised out of the garment. The Queen makes no expression. A gaggle of ladies in waiting and maidservants hand jewels, brooches and various pieces of the Queen's garb to Mrs Tuck who expertly puts these on. Over all of this we hear Ponsonby outline the days activities..

PONSONBY
(*voice-over*)

Breakfast with the Royal Princes of Belgium. An audience with the Sultan of Dubai where you will be presented with the Diamond of Ooojay. The garden party where you will receive the Right Honourable Marharani of Cooch Behar, Huran Singh, the Maharajah of Karpurthala . . .

INT. THE SAME, THE QUEEN'S BREAKFAST ROOM

The Queen is eating a goose egg with a silver spoon. Dr Reid and a phalanx of silent flunkeys are in attendance. Ponsonby is finishing his itinerary for the day:

PONSONBY

. . . And the Crown Princess Lili'uokalani.

QUEEN VICTORIA

Who on earth is she?

PONSONBY

Monarch and only Queen Regnant of the Kingdom of Hawaii, Your Majesty. She has composed a song for you on the ukelele – but we have managed to put her off. Then the afternoon audience with Prime Minister Salisbury.

DR REID

And your movements, Your Highness?

QUEEN VICTORIA

None to speak of.

DR REID

Not even during the day?

QUEEN VICTORIA

We last moved on Sunday evening.

DR REID

I fear the celebratory dinners are taking their toll. May I suggest some Benger's Mixture, Your Majesty?

QUEEN VICTORIA

I refuse to eat Benger's. It's baby food.

DR REID

But it is imperative, Your Majesty, that the royal colon receives a little roughage.

QUEEN VICTORIA

Is there anything else?

PONSONBY

Was Your Highness pleased with the mohar?

QUEEN VICTORIA

The what?

PONSONBY

The mohar. The ceremonial coin presented yesterday by the Indian servants.

QUEEN VICTORIA

I thought the tall one was terribly handsome.

INT. THE SAME, CORRIDOR

Arthur Bigge running at a surprising lick.

INT. SPIRAL STAIRCASE, ARSE END OF WINDSOR CASTLE

Bigge runs up to a door at the top. He throws it open. We see two small empty beds are crushed together.

EXT. COURTYARD. THE SAME

Abdul and Mohammed with their tiny suitcases are about to board a carriage. Arthur Bigge comes running breathlessly into the courtyard.

BIGGE

Stop!

He is almost doubled up with exhaustion. He catches his breath.

Slight change of plan.

Mohammed is horrified.

EXT. GARDEN PARTY. AFTERNOON

Abdul and Mohammed in costume. Bigge is in a food tent, guests mill around outside. They are near a table laden with puddings as they receive instructions.

BIGGE

You must not talk to any guests. Nod or bow but please do not interact with anybody other than the serving staff. I will come to you when the Queen is seated and you will present the pudding, as requested.

Abdul looks at the jelly on the table.

ABDUL
Excuse me, but what is it?

BIGGE
That is a jelly. A pudding made from the liquor of fruit.

Abdul and Mohammed survey it with great curiosity.

ABDUL
How do they get it so stiff?

BIGGE
Gelatin: a by-product of cow bone.

They look at the wobbling mass in horror.

MOHAMMED
Barbarians!

INT. QUEEN'S MARQUEE. WINDSOR CASTLE. DAY

The Queen is sitting at a table with Lord Salisbury.

LORD SALISBURY
There's another famine in India, more trouble in Ireland, I'm afraid. Suez is a perennial nightmare and I'm afraid the Boers are at it again.

QUEEN VICTORIA
Is there any good news, Prime Minister?

LORD SALISBURY
We have decided to annex Zululand, Your Majesty.

QUEEN VICTORIA
Whatever for?

LORD SALISBURY
To prevent the Transvaal having access to the sea.

QUEEN VICTORIA

Is that absolutely necessary?

LORD SALISBURY

We really have to box in the Boers if we possibly can, Your
Majesty.

QUEEN VICTORIA

Prime Minister, you really are terribly depressing.

Food starts to arrive.

Ah, luncheon!

EXT. THE SAME, TABLE AT THE GARDEN PARTY

*A wobbling jelly. We pull up to see Abdul carefully carrying it, followed
by Mohammed who has his own. Queen Victoria is at the table,
looking dour and fearsome. Abdul starts to panic as the jelly starts
wobbling perilously on the plate. The more he nears the Queen the
more errant the giant jelly becomes. With a great deal of sweat and
consternation Abdul navigates the jelly to Her Majesty.*

ABDUL

Jelly, Your Majesty.

*Abdul puts the jelly in front of the Queen, her eyes light up. Abdul
bows ostentatiously, then drops to his knees. The entire table of guests
crane round to see what he is doing. Bigge and Ponsonby look on in
horror. The Queen looks down curiously. The whole Royal Household
seem to hold their breath. Abdul suddenly lunges down – everyone
gasps. Kneeling down, he kisses her feet, rises, bows again and retreats
backwards. Everyone is astonished. The Queen is startled then her face
breaks into a smile.*

QUEEN VICTORIA

I feel a great deal better.

She picks up her golden spoon and looks at the jelly.

EXT. THE SAME, BEHIND THE FOOD TENT

An extremely red-faced Bigge has Abdul by the collar.

BIGGE

What the hell were you thinking?!

ABDUL

You said present the jelly.

BIGGE

I didn't say kiss the feet of the Empress of India.

ABDUL

I thought it would cheer her up.

PONSONBY

What on earth's going on here?! Her Majesty has requested Mr Karim and Mr Baksh to be her personal footmen for the rest of the Jubilee.

INT. STAIRCASE. WINDSOR CASTLE. DAY

Abdul and Mohammed follow Bigge up a staircase:

MOHAMMED

You stupid bloody idiot. All you had to do was give her jelly.

INT. OUTSIDE THE QUEEN'S WRITING ROOM. DAY

They've reached Ponsonby.

PONSONBY

Gentlemen. (*To Abdul.*) She wants you to stand by the writing desk. (*To Bigge.*) He can stand by the door.

INT. WRITING ROOM. THE SAME

Abdul stands to attention. The Queen is led in with ceremony. She sits down. Her pens are presented by a flunkey. The flunkey bows and goes off to stand by the door. Abdul is standing to attention right by her side, trying not to show his unease.

QUEEN VICTORIA

Don't worry. I'm not going to eat you.

The Queen takes a piece of headed notepaper and starts writing.

To Doctor Reid . . . A very successful movement . . . this
morning at eight a.m. . . . .

INT. CORRIDOR, OUTSIDE THE WRITING ROOM

*Bigge, various Ladies in Waiting and the two flunkeys. They are trying
to look through the keyhole.*

BIGGE

What's he doing?

INT. WRITING ROOM. THE SAME

*The Queen is deeply absorbed in her letter writing. She signs the letter
with a flourish. Then suddenly she is surprised by Abdul who appears
at her shoulder with a blotter. He blots her writing and smiles at her.*

QUEEN VICTORIA

Thank you, Mr . . .

ABDUL

Abdul. Abdul Karim. I am always writing. In India. I'm
writing all the day, every day.

QUEEN VICTORIA

Really. So in India you're not a servant.

ABDUL

No. In India I am writing in my very big book.

QUEEN VICTORIA

You're writing a book!

ABDUL

Oh yes. I am writing every name, who they are, what they
will be. This is my life. Every day I am writing. From the
morning to the night.

QUEEN VICTORIA

And this is fiction?

ABDUL

No, this is true. Everything I write is the very truth.

QUEEN VICTORIA

I don't understand, if you are an author why you are here, presenting the . . . thing, the . . .

ABDUL

The mohar. It is my humble privilege to serve Her Majesty. I was the one who chose your carpets.

QUEEN VICTORIA

The carpets?

ABDUL

For the exhibition. The Viceroy asked Mr Tyler but actually it was me. You have to have very good eye for the carpets. This is a very nice one. For example.

They look at the carpet beneath them.

ABDUL

Very tight knots. This is the sign of a very nice carpet. The art of carpets came to India with the great Emperor Akbar. The skill of a great carpet is to bring all the different threads together and we weave something we can stand on.

QUEEN VICTORIA

You seem to know an awful lot about it.

ABDUL

My family were carpet makers. But now I write in the book. Life is like the carpet. We weave in and out to make a pattern.

QUEEN VICTORIA

How very true. That is a very beautiful image.

ABDUL

It is a very beautiful carpet. Look at this – here is a bird of freedom caught forever in the design.

QUEEN VICTORIA

So in India you are a poet?

                    ABDUL
No. I just make a ledger of the prisoners.

                QUEEN VICTORIA
Indeed we are all prisoners.

                    ABDUL
Indeed we are, Your Majesty.

INT. THE SAME, ANTEROOM

Lady Phipps is listening at the door.

                LADY PHIPPS
Apparently he's a poet!

                    BIGGE
A poet?!

*Suddenly the doors burst open, out comes the Queen followed by
Abdul. Mohammed hisses in Hindi:*

                  MOHAMMED
What the hell are you playing at?

INT. ABDUL AND MOHAMMED'S CELL. NIGHT

A tiny room with two beds squashed together. Mohammed is shivering.

                    ABDUL
I was just trying to be friendly.

Abdul is breathing out, fascinated by his breath freezing.

                  MOHAMMED
Stop being friendly.

                    ABDUL
She's a very nice person.

                  MOHAMMED
She is the tyrannical oppressor of our entire country.
And if we don't get out of here we'll die of bloody cold.

Mohammed wraps himself in his blanket and turns away. Abdul carries on blowing out frozen exhalations.

MOHAMMED

Will you stop doing that!

EXT. GARDENS. WINDSOR CASTLE. DAY

Ponsonby with Dr Reid and Lady Churchill are hiding behind some trees so they can spy on the Queen and Abdul. Ponsonby looks through binoculars.

PONSONBY

You realise this is the third day in a row.

EXT. CANOPIED WRITING STATION. WINDSOR CASTLE. DAY

The Queen finishes writing. Abdul blots her copy. She closes the book. He goes back to 'standing sentry'. Then the Queen turns her attention directly to him.

QUEEN VICTORIA

So Mr Abdul. May I ask you which part of India are you from?

ABDUL

I am from Agra. The Taj Mahal. You have been to the Taj Mahal?

QUEEN VICTORIA

No.

ABDUL

Oh, it is the most marvellous building in the entire world. The Crown of Palaces. It was built by Shah Jahan, the grandson of the great Akbar, to remember his dead wife, Mumtaz Mahal, who died in childhood with their fourteenth child.

QUEEN VICTORIA

Goodness.

ABDUL

He was so upset with grief. He brought the greatest architects from Persia and Afghanistan to build the Taj Mahal.

QUEEN VICTORIA

It certainly sounds like a handsome building. I would very much like to see it.

ABDUL

Oh, it is beautiful, Your Majesty. All white marble. And Mumtaz laid inside. All of that beauty for the dead Queen.

QUEEN VICTORIA

How romantic.

ABDUL

Oh yes. And he wrote a poem:
    'The sight of this building brings me sad sighs;
    The sun and the moon have tears in their eyes.'
But it makes everyone so happy. Agra is very beautiful. Shah Jahan built the Red Fort, the Gardens of Shalimar, and the Peacock Throne.

QUEEN VICTORIA

The Peacock Throne?

ABDUL

Oh, it was the most beautiful throne in all the world. A throne of gold with peacocks on it. And in the throne was the Koh-i-Noor. He would look at the Taj Mahal through the diamond.

QUEEN VICTORIA

But I have the Koh-i-Noor. I have it as a brooch.

ABDUL

Do you?!

QUEEN VICTORIA

It was given to me by the East India Company. It wasn't very shiny so Albert had it recut. So what happened to the Peacock Throne?

> ABDUL

I don't know, they smashed it up.

> QUEEN VICTORIA

How awful.

> ABDUL

Oh, they are always smashing things up. All the British soldiers have taken the jewels from the Taj Mahal.

> QUEEN VICTORIA

British soldiers?!

> ABDUL

Oh yes, after the Mutiny.

> QUEEN VICTORIA

But this is terrible.

> ABDUL

At least you have the diamond.

EXT. GARDENS. WINDSOR CASTLE. DAY

Dr Reid looking through the binoculars.

> DR REID

What can they be talking about? An Indian and a servant to boot.

Lady Churchill grabs the binoculars.

> PONSONBY

What on earth does she see in him?

We see Abdul from Lady Churchill's point of view.

> LADY CHURCHILL

Well, he is rather handsome.

EXT. THE SAME, AVENUE OF TREES

Queen Victoria continues talking to Abdul as they walk.

QUEEN VICTORIA

But what happened to Shah Jahan?

ABDUL

He was overthrown by his son and died in Agra Fort.

QUEEN VICTORIA

The wickedness of children.

ABDUL

They buried him in the Taj Mahal next to his wife. They put an inscription: 'Here lies Shah Jahan who left this world to the Banquet Hall of Eternity.'

QUEEN VICTORIA

The Banquet Hall of Eternity.

ABDUL

Oh yes, it is a banquet when we leave here.

QUEEN VICTORIA

I rather like that idea. You seem very well informed, Mr Abdul.

ABDUL

Oh, these are famous stories in Uttar Pradesh. You should go there.

QUEEN VICTORIA

Oh, I can never go there. I am forbidden.

ABDUL

Forbidden?

QUEEN VICTORIA

They fear I would be assassinated.

ABDUL

But you are the Empress of India.

QUEEN VICTORIA

Exactly. (*Proudly.*) You know I've been shot at four times. And someone came for me with a knife!

ABDUL

Goodness. So you have never seen an India street, or a stall
of spices.

QUEEN VICTORIA

No.

ABDUL

Oh, the spices. Cardamom, turmeric, cumin, coriander.
Garam masala.

QUEEN VICTORIA

What is garam masala?

ABDUL

It's what you put into the sauce. You have never tasted
Indian food? A dahl? A rogan josh? Oh they are the greatest
dishes in the world! Biryani with mango chutney?

QUEEN VICTORIA

Mango chutney?

ABDUL

Oh yes, a chutney made of mango.

QUEEN VICTORIA

A mango?

ABDUL

Oh, the mango is the Queen of Fruit.

QUEEN VICTORIA

What does it taste like?

ABDUL

A mango is the most delicious fruit in all the world. Like an
orange and a peach.

INT. CORRIDOR. THE SAME

*Ponsonby and the ladies in waiting are accompanying Queen Victoria
down the corridor. Abdul and Mohammed in tow.*

QUEEN VICTORIA
Ponsonby. I would like a mango.

PONSONBY
A mango?

QUEEN VICTORIA
Yes, I would like to taste a mango.

PONSONBY
It's impossible. They only grow in India, Your Majesty.

QUEEN VICTORIA
I am the Empress of India, so have one sent. I hope you
will like Scotland, Abdul.

EXT. TOP OF THE MOOR. SCOTLAND. DAY

*Scottish mists. The vast landscape of Scotland. A train of flunkies
come into shot carrying tables, chairs, carpets. Ponsonby, Lady
Churchill, Miss Phipps and Reid struggle up with them. Queen
Victoria comes into view close to the camera. She points a finger.*

QUEEN VICTORIA
Here!

EXT. WILD PROMONTORY. DAY

*Queen Victoria is sitting at her 'tea' table, formally set up and replete
with every unnecessary accoutrement. It overlooks spectacular scenery,
but Queen Victoria behaves as if she was in her back garden. Abdul
and Mohammed stand to attention in the background. Mohammed
sneezes. Butlers and maids serve the tea. Queen Victoria is very well
wrapped up. She gorges herself on a sponge cake. Everyone else is cold
and miserable. Ponsonby whispers to Dr Reid:*

PONSONBY
It's alright for her. She's upholstered.

The hand of the serving man shakes as he pours the tea.

QUEEN VICTORIA
How do you like your new Scottish costumes?

ABDUL

They're very scratchy, Your Majesty.

QUEEN VICTORIA

Everything in Scotland is scratchy. (*To Ponsonby.*) When does Bertie come?

PONSONBY

Tomorrow, Your Majesty. He is on his way from Monte Carlo.

The Queen takes a slurp of the tea then puts the cup on the table. Suddenly there's a splish in the teacup. Then a pitter-pat as rain hits the table cloth.

EXT. VICINITY OF THE WILD PROMONTORY. SCOTLAND. DAY

Torrential rain. Queen Victoria is being led along by a river by a ghillie with an umbrella. Behind her, Abdul and Mohammed, Ponsonby and Reid are all getting soaked.

DR REID

I hate Scotland.

INT. THE SAME, BALMORAL

A piper plays very close to Dr Reid and Ponsonby who both blow their noses and wince at the infernal racket. It seems everyone now has a cold. The Household are sitting round in misery. The Queen is seated at the centre and is tapping her foot delicately as one of the ghillies is doing a dance in front of her. There is forced merriment from the staff. Mohammed and Abdul are standing at the side, watching the proceedings.

GHILLIE

(*in incomprehensible Scots*)
Ye must be the Hindoos. Very nice to meet ye.

Incomprehension from Abdul and Mohammed.

GHILLIE

Ye must be the Hindoos. Ye. Must. Be. The. Hin. Doos.

35

The piping stops.

QUEEN VICTORIA

More! More!

GHILLIE

I wish she'd bloody well go to bed.

The Ghillie wearily knocks back a dram from his hip flask. The piping starts again. Lady Phipps yawns. The unfortunate dancing Ghillie wearily raises his arms for another reel.

INT. STAFF CORRIDOR. NIGHT

Abdul and Mohammed walk to bed. Ahead of them is a butler, with a tray, careering from wall to wall. They pass an open door and inside see the kitchen staff with bottles of whisky open and someone playing the fiddle. Suddenly the music stops. They all look at Abdul and Mohammed looking in at them. The door closes. Abdul and Mohammed look at the closed door. The strathspey starts up again.

INT. QUEEN'S STUDY. DAY

The Queen is sitting at her desk, Abdul by her side. A servant comes in and puts down the boxes. Ponsonby blows his nose and takes her through it.

PONSONBY

Your boxes.

QUEEN VICTORIA

Thank you.

PONSONBY

And the blank journal you requested.

Ponsonby puts on his glasses and takes a pen out of his pocket ready to get down to work.

QUEEN VICTORIA

You may go.

Ponsonby waits. He is confused.

QUEEN VICTORIA

I am perfectly capable of working through the boxes. Abdul is very helpful with his blotter.

PONSONBY

But these are parliamentary papers, Your Majesty.

QUEEN VICTORIA

I am aware of that.

PONSONBY

But Abdul is a servant. He cannot assist with the boxes.

QUEEN VICTORIA

I am the Queen of England. I will have whatever help with my boxes that I require.

Ponsonby is completely banjaxed by the turn of events.

INT. THE SAME, OUTSIDE THE QUEEN'S ROOM

Ponsonby emerges wiping his brow. Mohammed is standing outside the room, as is Lady Churchill. They look to Ponsonby to discover the royal news.

PONSONBY

He's helping her with the boxes.

INT. THE SAME, QUEEN'S STUDY

Now the Queen and Abdul are alone she turns to him.

QUEEN VICTORIA

I want you to teach me Indian.

ABDUL

Indian?

QUEEN VICTORIA

Hindu. Whatever it is you speak.

ABDUL

Are you sure?

37

QUEEN VICTORIA

Of course I am sure.

ABDUL

But why would you want to speak Hindi?

QUEEN VICTORIA

I am Empress of India. Look. I have ordered a book. I want
you to give me private lessons.

ABDUL

I can't teach you Hindi.

QUEEN VICTORIA

Why ever not?

ABDUL

You are the Empress of India. You must learn Urdu. The
language of the Mughals. Oh there are a thousand
languages in India but Urdu is the most noble. The
difference is when you write it down. In Urdu you write
like this.

He demonstrates it.

This is Persian script. Just like Arabic. And for Hindi you
write like this – in Devanagari:

He demonstrates.

The Persian script is most superior.

QUEEN VICTORIA

I see.

ABDUL

I am the Queen. Mairn raini hoom.

QUEEN VICTORIA

Er donny hoo.

ABDUL

Mairn raini hoom.

QUEEN VICTORIA

Hey Donnneee whoo.

38

ABDUL

Whoom –

QUEEN VICTORIA

Hoowm.

INT. CORRIDOR. THE SAME

The gaggle of Ladies in Waiting and members of the Household has got bigger and they are listening outside, full of consternation.

LADY PHIPPS

He's teaching her Hindi!

MOHAMMED

Urdu, actually: the Muslim version.

They are aghast.

INT. QUEEN'S STUDY

ABDUL

Mairn raini hoom.

QUEEN VICTORIA

Mer ranee whoo.

ABDUL

That's it! That's it! You are the Queen.

He writes it down.

You see. Now you . . .

INT. CORRIDOR

Now Dr Reid has joined the group. He is looking through the keyhole.

REID

She's writing in the journal. And she's speaking in Hindustani.

PONSONBY

Urdu, actually. The Muslim version.

Mohammed raises an eyebrow.

INT. QUEEN'S STUDY

The Queen is laughing as she tries to repeat Abdul's phrase.

QUEEN VICTORIA

Apanni trishnup kili ap abdu tel new ad.

ABDUL

Nearly. Again.

QUEEN VICTORIA

Apanni trishnup kili ap abdu tel new ad.

ABDUL

Apni. Ni.

Abdul slaps his knees.

QUEEN VICTORIA

Knee. Knee.

ABDUL

Apani utkrsta sabaka kelie apa abdula dhan yavada. Thank you, Abdul, for your excellent lesson.

QUEEN VICTORIA

Apani utkrsta sabaka kelie apa abdula dhan yavada!

ABDUL

That's it. You did it. Now write it down.

INT. CORRIDOR, OUTSIDE THE WRITING ROOM

A new fat arse is on show as its owner bends in to look through the keyhole. The doors fly open. The arse stands up straight.

QUEEN VICTORIA

Bertie!

BERTIE

Mother!

QUEEN VICTORIA

Were you spying on me?

BERTIE

Were you learning Urdu?!

QUEEN VICTORIA

Yes, I was, as a matter of fact.

BERTIE

Do you think that's entirely appropriate?

QUEEN VICTORIA

I am the Empress of India. What could be more appropriate
than learning Urdu?

BERTIE

But in front of the entire Household –

QUEEN VICTORIA

You are absolutely right. I can't have all of these
distractions. Ponsonby, I wish to go to Glassalt Shiel.

BERTIE

Glassalt Shiel?!

Everybody is surprised. She looks at Bertie.

QUEEN VICTORIA

Alone.

BERTIE

But I've only just got here.

EXT. LOCHSIDE, DAY

*Drone shot of stunning scenery of the lochside. A tiny boat in the loch
moves towards a white cottage set against the lowering mountains
beyond.*

EXT. THE LITTLE HOUSE, GLASSALT SHIEL. DAY

Queen and Abdul on the promontory.

QUEEN VICTORIA

Oh, to be by oneself and live a simple rudimentary
existence.

She turns to Abdul.

QUEEN VICTORIA

They don't understand anything, those stupid aristocratic
fools. Toadying around. Jockeying for position. I've had this
my whole life. They couldn't bear me bringing dear John
Brown here. Yet I have been happier here than anywhere in
the entire world. Oh, I miss him, Abdul. And Albert. It's
been thirty years and I think about him every day. I am so
lonely, Abdul. Everyone I really loved has died. And I just
go on and on and on.

She weeps.

ABDUL

Oh, Your Majesty.

Abdul kneels and wipes her eyes.

QUEEN VICTORIA

It's an impossible position. No one really knows what it is
like to be Queen. I am hated by millions of people – all
over the world. I have had nine children, all vain and
jealous, and completely at loggerheads with each other.
Bertie is a complete embarrassment. I have thirty-four
grandchildren, my offspring will rule most of Europe – but
look at me: a fat, lame, impotent, silly old woman. What is
the point, Abdul?

ABDUL

The point, Your Majesty?

QUEEN VICTORIA

Of life?

ABDUL

Service.

QUEEN VICTORIA

Service?!

ABDUL

I think we are not here to worry about ourselves. We are
here to serve a greater purpose.

Queen Victoria thinks about this.

ABDUL

In the Koran it says: we are here for the good of others.

QUEEN VICTORIA

The Koran?

Abdul is trying to cheer up Her Majesty with his enthusiasm.

ABDUL

Oh yes, I am a Hafiz. I know the Koran by heart.

QUEEN VICTORIA

By heart. Isn't it very long?

ABDUL

There are 114 Surahs containing 6,236 verses.

QUEEN VICTORIA

And you know every word?

ABDUL

Many Muslim people know the Koran.

QUEEN VICTORIA

I thought you were a Hindu.

ABDUL

I am a Muslim, Your Majesty. I learnt the Koran from my father. And he taught me all the great poets: Kabir, Rumi. He is my Munshi.

QUEEN VICTORIA

Munshi?

ABDUL

Yes, Munshi. My teacher.

QUEEN VICTORIA

Then we would like you to be the Queen's Munshi.

ABDUL

But I am a servant. A servant cannot be a Munshi?

QUEEN VICTORIA

Well, you are a servant no longer. You are my teacher. You
shall teach me Urdu and the Koran and anything else you
think of.

INT. HALL. BALMORAL. NIGHT

*A dozen local guests are waiting for the dinner. Mohammed is
standing with a tray of sherry. Across the room Ponsonby, Bertie,
Miss Phipps, Lady Churchill and Dr Reid are gathered in a huddle.*

BERTIE

What the hell is a Munshi?

PONSONBY

Apparently it's some sort of 'spiritual teacher', Your Royal
Highness.

BERTIE

Has she completely lost her mind?! She's the head of the
Church of England, for God's sake! What's the Archbishop
of Canterbury going to say?

DR REID

It's utter lunacy.

LADY CHURCHILL

I say he's 'brown' John Brown.

DR REID

And what's more she's given him my room!

MISS PHIPPS

But where have they put you, Dr Reid?

DR REID
(*with a hateful look to Ponsonby*)

In the tower!

*Bertie suddenly sees the Queen arrive with Abdul in tow in his
magnificent Munshi garb.*

BERTIE

Oh my God.

Bertie looks horrified as the Queen approaches him.

> QUEEN VICTORIA
> Good evening, Bertie.

> BERTIE
> Mother?!

Aside Mohammed whispers to Abdul.

> MOHAMMED
> **What the hell are you wearing?**

Before Bertie can question Queen Victoria about this turn of events the Head Waiter announces:

> HEAD WAITER
> Dinner is served.

INT. THE SAME, STAIRCASE

Bertie with Queen Victoria.

> BERTIE
> Lady Churchill was absolutely scandalised. A servant. And a Hindoo to boot!

> QUEEN VICTORIA
> The Munshi is a Muslim scholar. He knows the Koran off by heart and for your information is no longer a servant. He is to be given a staff of his own.

> BERTIE
> This is absurd. Letters. Invitations to supper. You're treating him like family.

> QUEEN VICTORIA
> No, I like Abdul. Lady Churchill had better get used to the fact – as the Munshi is coming on holiday with us as a fully equal member of the Household.

> BERTIE
> You can't take a Muslim to Florence!

QUEEN VICTORIA

That will be all.

The Queen walks off upstairs.

INT. RAILWAY CARRIAGE. DAY

The train is trundling along. Mohammed blows his nose into his handkerchief.

MOHAMMED

A spiritual advisor!? You haven't an idea in your head. You promised to get us out of here. And now we're going to bloody Florence.

ABDUL

But don't you see what a privilege it is to see the glories of Italy with all these wonderful people?

MOHAMMED

You complete bloody idiot. Do you really think they are going to stand there and let her promote a wog? I did not come here to carry your bloody cases.

ABDUL

What you are complaining about? We have our own carriage. With a bathroom. They've a very nice bed for you on the floor.

Mohammed blows his nose.

MOHAMMED

I'm dying here. I want to go home. I am telling you this whole thing is a disaster waiting to happen.

ABDUL

I am getting sick of your negative attitude. Life is a big adventure. You just need to open up and enjoy it. We're on holiday. What on earth could possibly go wrong?

Abdul sees a rope above him – he grabs hold of it and reads the little sign beside it.

ABDUL

'Do Not Pull.'

INT. QUEEN'S CARRIAGE. TRAIN. LATER

The baroque splendour of the Queen's carriage. The Queen is in bed. Abdul is there.

ABDUL

I just want to apologise about the emergency brake, Your Majesty. I hope you weren't too badly injured.

QUEEN VICTORIA

It was nothing at all, Abdul. Anyway, it's a completely understandable mistake. I am just so glad you are with us. What a treat to show you Florence for the first time.

Bertie emerges from the royal bathroom in his pyjamas to see Abdul.

BERTIE

What's he doing here?

QUEEN VICTORIA

Abdul was just explaining what happened earlier.

BERTIE

I really don't see why I have to share your bathroom.

QUEEN VICTORIA

I shared a bed with my mother until I became Queen.

BERTIE

Mother, I am fifty-seven years old. The Munshi's got his own bathroom.

ABDUL

Oh yes, it is a very fine bathroom indeed, Your Majesty.

BERTIE

Excuse me.

He has to push his way past Abdul.

BERTIE

Goodnight, Ma-mah.

ABDUL

Goodnight, Mr Bertie.

QUEEN VICTORIA

Bertie. Make sure you shut that door.

Bertie pushes past Abdul unhappily and leaves. The Queen grabs Abdul's hand

QUEEN VICTORIA

Abdul, I have something for you. To celebrate your first trip to Florence. And becoming my Munshi. It is a locket. With a picture of me.

She gives him a locket.

ABDUL

Oh Your Majesty! How can I ever thank you.

QUEEN VICTORIA

Keep me safe.

ABDUL

For ever, Your Majesty.

QUEEN VICTORIA

Oh Abdul. You will love Florence. Such wonderful views.

INT. GARDENS, VILLA PALMIERI. DAY

Abdul and Queen Victoria are walking in the Italianate gardens below the terrace of the Villa Palmieri, Mohammed standing sentry in the background.

QUEEN VICTORIA

Isn't it glorious. Albert loved it here. The Brunelleschi Dome. The Uffizi Gallery. He spent all of his money on Old Masters. We collected so much I had to give most of it to the National Gallery. He so admired the Medicis. That they would commission the greatest artists of the day. So they could leave something astonishing behind.

ABDUL

In India we also commision great artists. Each Mughal Emperor would bring the greatest craftsmen to make great glories for their Durbar Room.

QUEEN VICTORIA

A Durbar Room?

ABDUL

Oh, yes, every Emperor had a Durbar Room. Full of the
finest things known to man.

QUEEN VICTORIA

Well, I am the Empress of India. I should have a Durbar
Room.

ABDUL

A brilliant idea, Your Majesty. But where would you put it?

QUEEN VICTORIA

The Isle of Wight. Obviously.

Ponsonby arrives.

PONSONBY

Signor Puccini has arrived, Your Majesty.

INT. GRAND ROOM. NIGHT

*We are in the middle of the recital. The Royal Household are listening
to a fat man singing 'Donna non vidi mai' at the piano. Abdul is
listening intently next to the Queen, Bertie next to Lady Churchill.
Ponsonby says something to Dr Reid. The Munshi turns:*

ABDUL

Ssshhhh!

*The fat man at the piano finishes his song. Abdul applauds
enthusiastically.*

QUEEN VICTORIA

And where did you say it was from, Mr Puccini?

PUCCINI

It's from my new opera *Manon Lescaut*. It's about two
lovers separated by the class divide who run away together.

QUEEN VICTORIA

It sounds marvellous.

PUCCINI

But she is imprisoned for her love, Your Majesty.

QUEEN VICTORIA

Oh.

PUCCINI

But they escape.

QUEEN VICTORIA

Bravo.

PUCCINI

But finally she dies, leaving him utterly bereft.

QUEEN VICTORIA

I'm not sure we do like the sound of it. We prefer comic opera. Do you know any Gilbert and Sullivan?

ABDUL

Perhaps Your Majesty will sing us a song?

QUEEN VICTORIA

Oh no. I couldn't possibly.

The Household on cue:

LADY CHURCHILL

But please, Your Majesty.

BERTIE
(*aside*)

God save us!

QUEEN VICTORIA

Well, just one. From *Pinafore*. Bertie.

BERTIE

Do I have to?

Bertie, reluctantly, goes to the piano.

QUEEN VICTORIA

'Little Buttercup'. In C.

Bertie sits at the piano with immense reluctance. Queen Victoria sings

'Little Buttercup' poorly. She dries, is about to continue, but Ponsonby prompts the applause.

ABDUL

Bravo! More! More!

But to everyone's relief Puccini produces a glass of champagne and hands it to the Queen.

PUCCINI

Bellissimo, Your Majesty.

QUEEN VICTORIA

I was taught by Mendelssohn, you know.

Puccini raises his glass.

PUCCINI

To the Queen.

QUEEN VICTORIA

To me.

She knocks back the champagne.

EXT. TERRACE, FLORENCE. NIGHT

The Queen is tipsy. She holds on to Abdul's arm as they walk along the terrace in the warm evening air, Florence twinkling below. Bertie and Lady Churchill look on aghast. The Queen is singing the melody of the Gilbert and Sullivan song:

QUEEN VICTORIA

La, la, la, la, la, la.

She lifts her arm as she walks, half dancing.

We should not have drunk all that champagne.

She giggles.

ABDUL

May I?

Abdul takes the Queen's other hand and they waltz their way along the terrace, 'la-la-ing' an accompaniment. We are close up on their almost childish pleasure. Finally the Queen and Abdul stumble and come to a stop. Abdul smiling at the Queen. Still holding her.

QUEEN VICTORIA
Abdul, I have not been so happy for years.

ABDUL
When I came to England, I was terrified of you. But you are a very kind lady. You are a very unique lady to me.

QUEEN VICTORIA
And you are very, very 'unique' to me, Abdul.

ABDUL
I know that you are very much older than me. And you are the Queen of England and Empress of India and I am just a humble Munshi. But I think you are the most special person in my whole life.

His eyes are alight. They look at each other intimately.

ABDUL
Even more special than my wife.

QUEEN VICTORIA
(*shocked*)

Wife?!

ABDUL

Yes.

The Queen is computing this information, her face severe.

QUEEN VICTORIA
You are married?!

ABDUL

Of course.

QUEEN VICTORIA
But where is your wife?

ABDUL

In India.

QUEEN VICTORIA
Why didn't you tell me you were married?

ABDUL

I didn't think it mattered.

QUEEN VICTORIA
(*severely*)

Of course, this changes everything. You will have to return to India immediately.

Abdul looks concerned.

And bring her back at once!

EXT. OSBORNE HOUSE. ISLE OF WIGHT. DAY

A shot of Osborne House. Huge music as a carriage approaches.

INT. THE SAME, QUEEN'S BEDCHAMBER

The Queen is sitting with her journal practising her Urdu.

QUEEN VICTORIA

Aaj kal Agra ka msusam kesa hay? [How is the weather in Agra these days?]

Mrs Tuck runs in.

MRS TUCK

He's coming!

INT. QUEEN'S DRESSING ROOM/BEDCHAMBER. DAY

The Queen passes a mirror, checks her appearance, then dashes out of the room.

EXT. OSBORNE HOUSE. DAY

A carriage races down the drive and into the circle in front of Osborne House.

INT. TOP OF THE STAIRS, OSBORNE HOUSE. DAY

Queen Victoria rushes past maids who jump to attention as she goes round a corner and dashes past Ponsonby and Dr Reid, who watch her whizz by in amazement.

EXT. OSBORNE HOUSE. DAY

The music of Triumphant Return continues as the carriage comes to a stand still. Mohammed is waiting by the door. He blows his nose.

MOHAMMED

Bloody hell.

And rushes towards the carriage to open the door.

INT. GLAZED TERRACE, OSBORNE HOUSE. DAY

The Queen is now looking out from the terrace with great anticipation.

QUEEN VICTORIA

How terribly exciting!

EXT. OSBORNE HOUSE. DAY

Mohammed runs, ignominiously, over the gravel to open the door of the carriage. We cut back to Osborne House. There are expectant faces at every window. The terrace is crowded with Household members. Mohammed opens the carriage door. Abdul emerges from the carriage. He steps down resplendent in his ceremonial outfit, double-sashed, replete with sword and pistol, and the Star of India. He looks like a cross between a Maharajah and a Pirate King and rather fatter than before. Mohammed is unimpressed.

MOHAMMED
(*under his breath*)

For God's sake!

INT. FIRST FLOOR TERRACE, OSBORNE HOUSE. DAY

Bertie, Lady Churchill, Miss Phipps are gathered with Alick Yorke, all looking down at Abdul's arrival.

LADY CHURCHILL

Look at the size of him.

BERTIE

And he's got a sword.

MISS PHIPPS

And a pistol!

EXT. OSBORNE HOUSE. THE SAME

*Abdul holds out his hand and Mrs Karim emerges from the carriage –
in full burqa.*

INT. FIRST FLOOR TERRACE, OSBORNE HOUSE. DAY

There is an audible gasp from Miss Phipps.

BERTIE
What the devil is she wearing?

MISS PHIPPS
You can't even see her face!

EXT. OSBORNE HOUSE. DAY

*A skinny serving boy, Ahmed, gets out of the carriage. He looks
around amazed at his surroundings.*

INT. FIRST-FLOOR TERRACE, OSBORNE HOUSE. DAY

*Now Dr Reid and Ponsonby are out on the terrace – further down
from Bertie and the Ladies in Waiting.*

DR REID
Who the hell is that?

EXT. OSBORNE HOUSE. DAY

Abdul cuffs Ahmed on the ear, bringing him 'to'.

ABDUL
The bags. The bags!

*Ahmed runs to help Mohammed with Mrs Karim's bags. Mrs Karim
stands resplendent.*

INT. GLAZED TERRACE. OSBORNE HOUSE. DAY

The Queen looks on delighted.

> QUEEN VICTORIA
> I think she looks rather splendid.

> MRS TUCK
> But you can't actually see her, Your Majesty.

> QUEEN VICTORIA
> I think it's rather dignified.

EXT. OSBORNE HOUSE. DAY

Abdul turns and helps another fully burqa'd lady from the carriage.

INT. FIRST FLOOR TERRACE, OSBORNE HOUSE. DAY

Another scandalised gasp from the company.

> LADY CHURCHILL
> Oh my God. Another one! How many has he got in there?

> BERTIE
> The ruddy sod's a bigamist!

> MISS PHIPPS
> (*delighted*)
> This is an absolute scandal!

EXT. OSBORNE HOUSE. DAY

*Abdul stands with his two burqua'd ladies while Mohammed and
Ahmed get bags from the carriage.*

INT. GLAZED TERRACE. OSBORNE HOUSE. DAY

The Queen looks on.

> QUEEN VICTORIA
> I do hope they like their little cottage.

INT. ABDUL'S COTTAGE. DAY

A knock at the door. Abdul opens the door to find the Queen.

QUEEN VICTORIA
I hope it's not inconvenient. I just thought we'd pop round
for tea.

EXT. OTTAGE. DAY

*A chocolate-box cottage on the Osborne Estate. We see the Queen is
accompanied by a vast entourage of people.*

INT. TINY LIVING ROOM, ABDUL'S COTTAGE. DAY

*A 'tableau' of Queen Victoria, Ponsonby, Lady Churchill, the Queen
of Greece (1870–1932), the Grand Duchess Sophie of Saxe-Weimar-
Eisenach (1824–97), Princess Helena of Schleswig-Holstein-
Sonderburg-Augustenburg (1848–1923), and their entourages,
Mohammed, Abdul, Ahmed, Mrs Karim and the mother-in-law along
with the usual entourage, plus the retinue of the royal visitors, all
squashed tightly in Abdul's tiny living room. Bertie and Dr Reid are
perched on travel cases because of the lack of chairs.*

QUEEN VICTORIA
This is my granddaughter, Sophia, The Queen of Greece,
this is the Grand Duchess Sophie of Saxe-Weimar-
Eisenach, and my daughter, Princess Helena Augusta
Viktoria of Schleswig-Holstein-Sonderburg-Augustenburg.

ABDUL
A pleasure to meet you. This is my wife Mrs Karim, and
this is my mother-in-law.

QUEEN VICTORIA
How very nice to meet you. How are you enjoying England,
Mrs Karim?

*Abdul translates this – at great length – to his missus. She whispers
something to him – also at great length, then . . .*

ABDUL
She says: 'Very well. Thank you, Your Majesty.'

The Munshi's wife then whispers to him again for an interminably
long time. Everyone waits politely. Finally he turns and smiles.

ABDUL

'Apart from the cold.'

They laugh gently.

BERTIE
(*aside*)

God help me.

ABDUL

Your Majesty, Sophia – the Queen of Greece, Grand
Duchess Sophie of Saxe-Weimar-Eisenach, Princess Helena
Augusta Viktoria of Schleswig-Holstein-Sonderburg-
Augustenburg, I would like to take this opportunity on
behalf of myself, my wife and my wife's mother to thank
Her Majesty Victoria Regina of the United Kingdom of
Great Britain and Ireland, Defender of the Faith, Empress
of India, for accommodating us in this beautiful cottage.
We are extremely grateful for her infinite kindness and
interior decoration. The gift of hospitality and friendship
to strangers is of very high importance in our culture and
we are honoured to repay it in our very small way. What is
ours is yours.

BERTIE
(*under his breath*)

Quite literally.

ABDUL

And this is how the world should be. Here we are,
representatives of the great nations of the world, all
snuggled together, having a nice cup of Indian tea. Thanks
be to Allah.

Queen Victoria leads the polite applause.

QUEEN VICTORIA

My dear Munshi, Mrs Karim and Mrs Karim's mother –
it's so good to have you back, my children. We have missed
you enormously.

EXT. ABDUL'S COTTAGE. DAY

A groom and pony-driven carriage wait for the Queen. The royal visitors are leaving. Bertie marches up the path, Ponsonby anxiously following close behind:

BERTIE

Children?!

Dr Reid is on Ponsonby's heels.

DR REID
(*aside, to Ponsonby*)
If they are going to live here can I get my room back?

The Queen is the last to leave. She takes his hand:

QUEEN VICTORIA

Oh Abdul, I am so glad you are back – it really has been dreadfully dull without you. And I am so glad to meet Mrs Karim. There's just one thing I've been curious about this whole afternoon. What does Mrs Karim look like behind her veil?

ABDUL

Behind her veil? You must see her.

QUEEN VICTORIA

Is that allowed?

ABDUL

Of course it is allowed. You are a lady. And the Empress of India.

QUEEN VICTORIA

Really?! You think she'd let me take a glimpse?

ABDUL

She would be honoured, Your Majesty.

Ponsonby and Bertie at the end of the garden path.

BERTIE

Where the hell is she going now?

INT. TINY LIVING ROOM, ABDUL'S COTTAGE. DAY

*Queen Victoria is sitting on a chair. Mrs Karim takes off her burqa.
We glimpse the gorgeous costume underneath, full of colour. Then we
see her face. Her nose is pierced with a gold chain linked to her ear.
She giggles like a schoolgirl. Victoria is transfixed.*

QUEEN VICTORIA
Oh, you really are beautiful.

*Mrs Karim giggles again, not understanding a word. The Queen
stands and takes both of her hands:*

QUEEN VICTORIA
Tum bahut sundar ho. [You are very beautiful.]

*Mrs Karim beams. Her mother watches inscrutably from her burqa.
Abdul looks on at the whole scene, proud as Punch.*

QUEEN VICTORIA
Main tum yahaan hai bahut khush hoon. [I am so happy
to have you here.]

EXT. OSBORNE HOUSE. DAY

*A carriage arrives. Ponsonby is waiting for Lord Salisbury, who
gets out.*

LORD SALISBURY
What on earth is a Durbar Room?

INT. OSBORNE, CORRIDOR APPROACHING DURBAR ROOM. DAY

*The Prime Minister, Lord Salisbury, is marching up a corridor,
followed by his private secretary and deputy private secretary, with a
face filled with fury. Bertie and Ponsonby are running alongside.*

PONSONBY
It is a celebration of all things Indian inspired by the
Mughal Emperors, Prime Minister.

LORD SALISBURY
But I don't understand. Who gave her permission to build
this in the first place?

BERTIE

Don't blame me. I was in Monte Carlo.

PONSONBY

I'm afraid she is a law unto herself, Prime Minister.

LORD SALISBURY

For God's sake. She'll be wearing a burqa next. I am
holding you entirely responsible, Ponsonby.

*They have arrived at the Queen, who is waiting with Dr Reid, Lady
Churchill, Miss Phipps and the usual entourage.*

QUEEN VICTORIA

Prime Minister, you are late.

LORD SALISBURY

I'm terribly sorry, Your Majesty.

QUEEN VICTORIA

Let us begin.

INT. INDIAN CORRIDOR. DAY

*The Queen leads Salisbury, Ponsonby, Bertie, etc. down the Indian
corridor.*

QUEEN VICTORIA

This, as you can see, is the Indian corridor. The Durbar
Room was designed by Mr Bhai Ram Singh.

They pass a smiling Mr Bhai Ram Singh.

BERTIE
(*in Salisbury's ear*)
The place is crawling with them.

QUEEN VICTORIA

And we commissioned a series of portraits. Of eminent
Indians. This is Princess Gurmma.

Lord Salisbury tries to feign interest as he looks at the painting.

QUEEN VICTORIA

This, of course . . . is the Munshi.

*Salisbury looks horrified at the portrait of Abdul. Then his eye falls
upon the real Abdul who is in full Munshi uniform, a flowing smock.*

Abdul beams at the Prime Minister.

> ABDUL
> An honour to meet you, Mr Prime Minister, sir.

> QUEEN VICTORIA
> A very good likeness. Don't you think?

> ABDUL
> (*whispering to Lord Salisbury*)
> I asked him to take a few pounds off. This is my wife, Mr
> Prime Minister, sir, and this is my mother-in-law.

The two ladies are by his side in their identical burqas.

> At least I think that's the right way round.

Abdul chuckles at his own joke.

> And this is my servant, Mohammed.

Mohammed blows his nose. Ahmed is there.

> LORD SALISBURY
> (*aside to Ponsonby*)
> What the hell is going on here, Ponsonby?

> QUEEN VICTORIA
> And this, Prime Minister, is the Durbar Room.

INT. DURBAR ROOM, CONTINUOUS

*Salisbury follows the Queen into the Durbar Room in all its splendour.
It is a state room decorated in an over-the-top higgledy-piggle of
Mughal and Hindu motifs. Indian musicians play from the balcony.
The Queen walks through the room pointing out the carvings:*

> QUEEN VICTORIA
> The carvings are all from Uttar Pradesh.

And the carpet:

> The carpet was woven in a gaol in Agra. Perfect, of course,
> for the tableaux.

At the end of the room is the Peacock Throne.

QUEEN VICTORIA
And the *pièce de résistance*. The Peacock Throne.

The Queen sits on the throne.

An exact copy of the one in Agra. And, of course, the
Koh-i-Noor!

She is wearing the Koh-i-Noor brooch.

QUEEN VICTORIA
Now I really do feel like the Empress of India.

*She is like a little child, swinging her feet joyously. Salisbury and the
household deputation look on at her:*

BERTIE
(*aside to Dr Reid*)
I thought she was supposed to be dying.

LORD SALISBURY
It really is a remarkable addition to the house, Your
Majesty.

QUEEN VICTORIA
We have Abdul to thank for the whole idea.

ABDUL
(*who is now standing next to the Queen*)
Oh, really – it was nothing.

Ponsonby steps forward, very formally.

PONSONBY
To celebrate the completion of the Durbar Room. A little
surprise, Your Majesty.

*Mohammed appears bearing an ornately inlaid box. The Queen opens
the box and looks inside. Pulling a confused face:*

QUEEN VICTORIA
What is it?

PONSONBY
A mango, Your Majesty.

A general gasp. Abdul peers inside.

ABDUL

It's 'off'.

A look of horror on everyone's face.

QUEEN VICTORIA

Ponsonby. This mango is off.

Ponsonby's chagrin.

INT. LADIES' DRESSING ROOM, OSBORNE HOUSE. NIGHT

Lady Churchill, Miss Phipps, and various other ladies from the entourage in petticoats getting undressed. Helped by Mrs Tuck.

LADY CHURCHILL

A line has definitively been crossed.

INT. MEN'S DRESSING ROOM. OSBORNE HOUSE. NIGHT

Abdul is getting changed into his Sultan of Persia outfit. Mohammed wipes his brow and sits down, shaking with a fever.

MOHAMMED

This is a complete and utter disaster.

ABDUL

I don't understand.

MOHAMMED

They've been waiting for this.

ABDUL

Who have?

MOHAMMED

Ponsonby, Reid. The whole damn lot of them. Don't you see, she's been rubbing their noses in it but now it's going public. I'm telling you they're not going to stand for it – they'll rise up and chop your bloody balls off. You've upset the order of everything. You think they are going to lie back and take it?

ABDUL

But I haven't done anything.

MOHAMMED

You stupid, bloody Uncle Tom. Don't you see you've upset the order of everything. I'm telling you this whole thing is a complete catastrophe.

Abdul looks worried.

ALICK YORKE

Everything alright in here?

INT. DURBAR ROOM. NIGHT

Now the Durbar Room has been transformed. A large stage with a plush velvet curtain has been erected at one end and dominates the room. The room is crammed with people ready to see the tableaux. Bigge, Reid, Ponsonby, all the staff in the rear rows crane to see the arrival of Mrs Karim and Mrs Karim's mother.

The Queen raises her hand and waves at Mrs Karim.

QUEEN VICTORIA

Mrs Munshi! Please, sit here. Bertie.

Bertie, much put out, is forced to move. Salisbury watches the whole thing in horror.

INT. LADIES' DRESSING ROOM. NIGHT

Lady Churchill puts on her a yashmak and looks in the mirror.

LADY CHURCHILL

I have never been so humiliated in my entire life.

INT. DURBAR ROOM. NIGHT

The lights in the hall have dimmed. Music. The Queen squeezes Mrs Karim's hand. Alick Yorke appears from between the curtains on stage.

ALICK YORKE

A scene in Ancient Persia.

He withdraws. Ponsonby pops a pill. The Queen is agog with delighted anticipation. The curtains open to reveal painted flats. A scene from Ancient Persia. Lady Churchill, Miss Phipps and Mrs Tuck come on dressed in Persian costumes. They pose as a harem of supplicants. Enter Abdul, dressed as the Sultan of Persia with Ahmed as his servant. Mohammed is at the back sick with fever.

ABDUL

I am the Sultan of Persia, King of all Kings. You are now under my power.

LADY CHURCHILL

Your Highness. We bestow all the riches of the Orient upon you.

The ladies proffer paste jewels. Abdul tries his best to look triumphantly regal. They all look out uneasily at the audience trying to maintain a matey rictus as the orchestra swells and they hold the tableau. Ahmed is in the way – Abdul surreptitiously cuffs him to clear his sightline.

We notice Mohammed swaying, clearly ill, and just as the curtain descends as everyone else is fixed in the tableau, Mohammed sneezes. Lord Salisbury is open-mouthed. Ponsonby holds his forehead in despair. The Queen is unabashed with her approval.

QUEEN VICTORIA

Bravo! Bravo the Munshi!

BERTIE

(*aside to Dr Reid*)

Now she thinks he's Henry Irving.

As the curtain opens for the 'call', the Queen leaps to her feet. The entire household follow suit, applauding politely. Only Mrs Karim and her mother remain seated. Abdul gestures his respects to Her Majesty and bows egregiously. She claps enthusiastically. The curtains close again. Salisbury is not happy.

INT. HALLWAY, OSBORNE HOUSE. NIGHT

Lord Salisbury bollocks Ponsonby.

LORD SALISBURY

What the hell is this, Ponsonby? Munshi-mania? I'm trying

to keep an empire together and it looks like they're running the place. I want this whole sodding mess knocked on the head or you're finished. Understood?

Lord Salisbury turns and leaves leaving Ponsonby chagrined.

INT. POST-TABLEAU ROOM, OSBORNE HOUSE. NIGHT

The post-tableau soirée. Victoria is sitting amongst the prominent members of the household, drinking sherry. Ponsonby, battle-torn, comes in to join them.

> QUEEN VICTORIA
> Ah, Ponsonby. Tell us, what exactly did the Prime Minister say about the tableau?

> PONSONBY
> To be entirely frank, Your Majesty, he seemed to be a little perturbed.

> QUEEN VICTORIA
> Whatever for? He must have liked the Munshi.

> PONSONBY
> I think the Munshi was the problem, Your Majesty.

> QUEEN VICTORIA
> Really? I thought he was rather good.

> PONSONBY
> I think he meant his position, Your Majesty. I think he was rather alarmed he had such a prominent role in the Household.

> QUEEN VICTORIA
> Of course Abdul has a prominent role in the household. He is my Munshi.

> PONSONBY
> But he's an Indian, Your Majesty.

> QUEEN VICTORIA
> I am aware of it.

PONSONBY

But given current sensitivities in the sub-continent, Your Majesty. The Prime Minister was concerned it might be 'sending the wrong message'.

QUEEN VICTORIA

I should have thought it was a jolly good message.

PONSONBY

But he's a Muslim, Your Majesty.

QUEEN VICTORIA

Precisely. We owe them so much, do we not? For their role in the Mutiny, for example.

The hubbub drops to a deathly silence.

PONSONBY

The Mutiny, Your Majesty?

QUEEN VICTORIA

Yes. For all the help they gave us with the Hindus.

DR REID

But the Mutiny was a Muslim-led revolt, Your Majesty.

QUEEN VICTORIA

Are you sure?

DR REID

Of course. The Muslim soldiers revolted when it was rumoured their rifles were greased with pork fat.

QUEEN VICTORIA

Really?

PONSONBY

The Grand Mufti, himself, put out a fatwa against you personally. And Muslim soldiers killed over two thousand British personnel.

BERTIE

Who have you been talking to, Mother?

Suddenly Abdul arrives with a flourish in his smartest Munshi garb.

ABDUL

Ta-da!

The Queen glares at him. Everyone else is staring. He realises something is wrong.

INT. SCULPTURE CORRIDOR. OSBORNE HOUSE. NIGHT

The Queen is standing next to Abdul in the corridor, giving him a furious dressing down.

QUEEN VICTORIA

I have opened my heart to you. I have brought your family from India, promoted you in the teeth of very considerable opposition and disquiet from the Household. I even turned a blind eye when you failed to tell me you were married, which came, as you know, as quite a surprise. How could you let me humiliate myself in front of the entire Household?

ABDUL

I am deeply sorry, Your Majesty.

QUEEN VICTORIA

You said the Hindus were behind the Mutiny!

ABDUL

I didn't say it was only the Hindus, Your Majesty.

QUEEN VICTORIA

You told me categorically that the Muslims were my friends.

ABDUL

But we are your friends, Your Majesty.

QUEEN VICTORIA

Abdul, there is a fatwa against me. It was Muslims who started the whole thing! This is completely unacceptable. Abdul, I thought you were outstanding as the Sultan of Persia, but I'm afraid you will have to go home.

INT. FURTHER ALONG THE CORRIDOR. NIGHT

Bertie, Lady Churchill and Dr Reid have gathered and are spying on the conversation. Unable to repress his delight:

> DR REID
> Hallelujah!

INT. OSBORNE HOUSE. SCULPTURE CORRIDOR

Abdul is knocked for six.

> QUEEN VICTORIA
> You have hurt my feelings very much indeed, Abdul. Don't you see what a position I have been put in? Thank you for everything you've done for me.

She starts to leave. She turns and faces Abdul. We can see Mohammed looking on behind her.

> I will miss you a very great deal.

She turns and walks down the corridor.

Queen Victoria marches along the corridor passing Bertie, Dr Reid and Lady Churchill, who dutifully follow her, smirking like cats that have got the cream.

Abdul is standing devastated. We see Mohammed has been watching.

> MOHAMMED
> So we're going home.

He starts to cough.

INT. SCULPTURE CORRIDOR. NIGHT

Victoria walks along the corridor followed by the smirking Bertie, Dr Reid and Lady Churchill. The Queen stops at the end stairs, met by Mrs Tuck. Victoria turns to face Bertie, Reid and Churchill. They suddenly adopt an appropriately solemn demeanour.

> BERTIE
> Goodnight, Mother.

QUEEN VICTORIA
Goodnight.

The Queen eyes them suspiciously – she knows she's been had. They try to keep straight faces.

INT. STAIRS. THE SAME

The Queen turns and struggles up the stairs. Reid's face breaks into a smile.

INT. QUEEN'S BEDCHAMBER. OSBORNE HOUSE. NIGHT

The Queen on her dressing stool, unnerved. She looks up at the photo of Abdul on her wall: Abdul standing proudly as she sits at her desk. She thinks.

QUEEN VICTORIA
Mrs Tuck!

INT. ABDUL'S COTTAGE. NIGHT

Pouring rain. It is Mrs Tuck under an umbrella. Abdul is amazed.

EXT. LANE OUTSIDE. NIGHT

Victoria is in her pony and trap. Abdul is standing by the trap under an umbrella held by Mrs Tuck.

QUEEN VICTORIA
Abdul, you have been an utter fool and I am absolutely furious with you. It is unconscionable that as my Munshi you should have lied to me in any way. But also it would be completely churlish not to recognise the considerable kindness and devotion you've shown. And after all, I am sure you thought in some way you were protecting me. But as the monarch, I do realise nothing can really protect me. And in that light I have decided, even though I am very disappointed, I would like you to stay.

Abdul is astonished.

QUEEN VICTORIA
But it must never happen again.

ABDUL
Oh Your Gracious Majesty. How can I ever thank you?

QUEEN VICTORIA
Well, there is something we really must sort out, Abdul.

Abdul has no idea what she could mean.

I am deeply concerned about Mrs Karim.

INT. QUEEN'S BEDROOM. OSBORNE HOUSE. DAY

The Queen is having breakfast in bed attended by Dr Reid, Ponsonby and Mrs Tuck.

QUEEN VICTORIA
I want you to examine Mrs Karim.

DR REID
Examine Mrs Karim?!

QUEEN VICTORIA
Just make sure everything's working.

PONSONBY
But I thought the Munshi and his family were leaving us, Your Majesty.

QUEEN VICTORIA
Whatever gave you that impression?

Astonishment from all and sundry.

The Munshi and his family are an integral part of the Royal Household. And I would be very grateful if you gave her a thorough examination.

She blithely goes back to work on her egg. Dr Reid looks at Ponsonby.

INT. OSBORNE HOUSE. TOP OF STAIRS. DAY

Bertie, Ponsonby and Reid descending the stairs.

BERTIE

As far as I'm concerned this is war. We're going to dig up
every last piece of shit the blaggard's ever done. I want
someone in India raking through the family coals. Isn't
your son out there, Ponsonby?

PONSONBY

I couldn't possibly be involved in subterfuge, Your Majesty.

BERTIE

Look. I'm going to be the one in charge very soon. You'll
do as you're bloody well told. I want no stone unturned.
We are going to make a dossier. Have it all down in black
and white; and put an end to this for good.

Bertie leaves. Ponsonby looks at Dr Reid.

DR REID

Well, I better go and examine Mrs Munshi.

INT. COTTAGE. DAY

*Dr Reid is sitting awkwardly on a chair, a stethoscope round his neck,
clearly very unhappy. The Munshi's wife is in full burqa with a veil,
sitting on the side of the bed. Her mother, also in full burqa, sits beside
her holding her hand. Dr Reid looks at Mrs Karim awkwardly, then
turns to Abdul who is waiting anxiously by the doctor's side.*

REID

I need to see her tongue.

ABDUL

Oh, it is not possible to uncover a lady's mouth, Doctor.

REID

But how can I tell anything if I can't see her tongue?

*Abdul speaks to the mother-in-law in Hindi, the mother-in-law speaks
to Mrs Karim. Then she daintily lifts her yashmak a fraction and
sticks out her tongue. The doctor looks at it gingerly then it disappears
back behind the veil as quickly as it appeared.*

ABDUL

Well?

I think she's fine.

INT. OUTSIDE MOHAMMED'S ROOM. DAY

Ponsonby and Bertie are in the servants' corridor. Ponsonby knocks on a door.

INT. MOHAMMED'S ROOM. DAY

Bertie and Ponsonby are in Mohammed's room. Mohammed has declined since we last saw him.

PONSONBY

Mr Mohammed. We have come here because we are not unaware of your predicament. That you arrived in the first place almost by accident and find yourself stuck here through a bizarre set of circumstances – none of your own making. It is not beneath our notice that the inclement English weather, especially on the Solent, has been the cause of a precipitous decline in your general health and what's more you continue to suffer the vast indignity of being a servant to someone who is in many ways your inferior, who seems to discharge his role with increasing abuse and disregard. But it has occurred to us that we might be able to offer you some help.

MOHAMMED

Help?

PONSONBY

Travel home, medical care, perhaps a modest pension. In return, of course, for a little information.

MOHAMMED

What sort of information?

PONSONBY

Look, I'm not going to beat about the bush. You've borne the brunt of Abdul's appalling behaviour and that is of a great deal of interest to a lot of people.

MOHAMMED

You want me to dish the dirty?

PONSONBY

In a manner of speaking.

Mohammed coughs into his handkerchief.

MOHAMMED

What would you like me to say?

BERTIE

Anything really.

PONSONBY

We need details. What he says, what he does.

Mohammed thinks about this.

MOHAMMED

Abdul does what everybody else does. Looks for preferment. 'Curries' favour. Crawls up the stinking greasy pole of the shitty British Empire. Making fools of you all because he is a servant — an Indian, Muslim servant – and you are all quaking in your boots because he's beating you at your own game.

BERTIE

No one is quaking in their boots. We are the most powerful nation on Earth at the height of our influence.

MOHAMMED

In that case the only way is down. So stick your stupid British Empire up your stinky royal bottom-hole, Mr Bertie Prince, sir. I hope he makes the whole damn thing come tumbling down.

He coughs into his handkerchief. There is blood. Mohammed is shocked. Ponsonby looks on in pity.

BERTIE

I'll see that you die here.

INT. OSBORNE HOUSE. COUNCIL CORRIDOR. DAY

Bertie and Ponsonby in a cabal with Dr Reid.

DR REID
What do you mean, he wouldn't say anything?

PONSONBY
Well . . .

BERTIE
The man's a complete shit.

QUEEN VICTORIA
(*out of shot*)

Dr Reid!

The Queen comes round the corner. Suddenly Ponsonby et al. swing round to see her with Lady Churchill, Miss Phipps et al.

QUEEN VICTORIA
I am not a fool. I know there is some skulduggery afoot. Something is going on here and I am not going to stand for it.

Ponsonby et al. look terrified.

QUEEN VICTORIA
Dr Reid, I asked you to get to the bottom of Mrs Karim's fertility issues and it seems nothing has been done.

DR REID
Well, actually, Your Majesty, it was impossible to make a conclusive judgement for religious reasons.

QUEEN VICTORIA
Well, did you examine the Munshi?

DR REID
No, Your Majesty.

QUEEN VICTORIA
Well, examine the Munshi.

The Queen heads off. Lady Churchill and Bertie hold back.

Bertie.

Bertie sheepishly follows. Dr Reid turns to Ponsonby.

> DR REID

I did not do seven years at Edinburgh University to look at Indian dicks.

EXT. OSBORNE HOUSE. DAY

Dr Reid stomps, unhappily, carrying his doctor's bag towards Abdul's house.

INT. ABDUL'S COTTAGE. DAY

Dr Reid with his stethoscope, as before. Abdul standing.

> DR REID

Trousers.

EXT. OSBORNE HOUSE. DAY

Dr Reid running at full pelt in the opposite direction.

EXT. COURTYARD. OSBORNE HOUSE. DAY

Dr Reid running across the courtyard.

INT. CORRIDOR. OSBORNE HOUSE

Dr Reid running. He skids round a corner.

INT. PONSONBY'S OFFICE. OSBORNE HOUSE. DAY

Reid bursts in.

> DR REID

Eureka!

Ponsonby looks up.

He's riddled with the clap!

INT. CORRIDOR. OSBORNE HOUSE. DAY

Ponsonby and Reid knock on a bedroom door. A voice from inside.

> BERTIE
> (*off*)

Go away!

> PONSONBY

Your Royal Highness. We come with important news about the Munshi!

INT. BERTIE'S BEDROOM. OSBORNE HOUSE. DAY

Bertie is now in bed with a post-coital cigar. Lady Churchill is also in the bed. Ponsonby and Dr Reid have just explained the news.

> BERTIE

The clap!

> LADY CHURCHILL

But we can't possibly tell her. It would kill her stone dead.

> BERTIE

Maybe it's not such a bad idea.

> PONSONBY

There's more. It appears the father, far from being an Indian Eminent, is in fact a prison apothecary.

> BERTIE

Are you sure?

> PONSONBY

I received a telegram only this afternoon from Agra. My son visited the gaol himself. They are absolute nobodies.

Bertie takes a puff while he thinks about this.

> BERTIE

Well, it sounds pretty conclusive to me.

INT. QUEEN'S STUDY. OSBORNE HOUSE. DAY

Bertie knocks on the door and goes in.

BERTIE

Mother, we have to see you . . .

The Queen is sitting behind a small desk, Abdul intimately by her side. Ponsonby and Dr Reid stand nervously before her.

BERTIE
(*looking at Abdul*)

Alone.

QUEEN VICTORIA

I am in the middle of my Urdu lesson.

BERTIE

Mother, we come with very important news of a highly personal matter.

QUEEN VICTORIA

I have nothing to hide from Abdul.

PONSONBY

I am afraid, Your Majesty, We have news concerning the Munshi. Proof, beyond any doubt, that Abdul Karim is a low-born imposter, Your Majesty.

QUEEN VICTORIA

But the Munshi is from a noble family and a long line of teachers.

PONSONBY

The Munshi was a mere clerk in a common gaol.

She is silent.

My own son has sent word from India and has actually spoken to the man in question.

DR REID

His family are completely uneducated. His father is a lowly apothecary.

BERTIE

The Munshi didn't even go to school, Mother. The man's a complete fraud. There he is, overseeing the boxes. I'm next in line and I can't get anywhere near them.

It is true, Your Majesty. You have been hideously duped and
ignominiously misused, Your Majesty. The Munshi is a
blackguard and an arch deceiver. I am afraid Abdul and his
father are completely common.

The Queen looks horrified at the proceedings.

We have prepared a dossier.

*Ponsonby flourishes the dossier and slams it on the Queen's table. She
seems flabbergasted. She looks at the dossier. The case seems conclusive.
They stare at her with bated breath.*

QUEEN VICTORIA

You despicable toads. Racialists! Spying?! Dossiers?!
Picking on a poor defenceless Indian. Of course they don't
have qualifications. It's completely different out there.

BERTIE

But don't you see, Mother, he's using his position for his
own gain.

QUEEN VICTORIA

And how does that make him any different to any one of
you? How dare you look down on Abdul. How dare you
defame his poor father. Bertie, I am ashamed that you are
part of this. Abdul is a loyal, wise, sympathetic human
being who has risen on his own merits. Not by endless
backstabbing or family connections. I will not have this.
Now. Repeat after me. I will be courteous to the Munshi.

She stares at Ponsonby. He looks at Abdul, then reluctantly:

PONSONBY

I will be courteous to the Munshi.

QUEEN VICTORIA

You.

DR REID

I will be courteous to the Munshi.

QUEEN VICTORIA

Bertie. All of you. 'I will be courteous to the Munshi.'

EVERYONE

I will be courteous to the Munshi.

QUEEN VICTORIA

It has become apparent that to get any respect in the
Household one needs to be formally recognised. In which
case, Abdul, I intend to give you a knighthood in the next
honours list.

Ponsonby almost collapses.

DR REID

Enough! This is absurd. We can't protect you from this any
further.

The Queen stares in astonishment.

The man is riddled with gonorrhoea.

Stunned silence.

QUEEN VICTORIA

Gonorrhoea!?

PONSONBY

Yes, Your Majesty.

QUEEN VICTORIA

Well, you're a doctor. Why don't you treat him?! Now get
out of my sight. All of you.

INT. OUTSIDE THE QUEEN'S STUDY. OSBORNE HOUSE. DAY

*Abdul, Bertie, Ponsonby and Reid come out of the room. Suddenly
Dr Reid loses it and pins Abdul up against the wall.*

REID

You're killing her, you pox-ridden Indian shit.

Reid is strangling Abdul.

ABDUL

Doctor R—

*Abdul turns puce as Reid throttles him. Ponsonby tries to wrest Abdul
from Dr Reid's clutches.*

PONSONBY

Dr Reid! Be courteous!

Reid comes to his senses and lets go. Abdul is shaken.

INT. PONSONBY'S OFFICE. OSBORNE HOUSE. NIGHT

*The council is completely full with scores of staff and members of the
Royal Household.*

LADY CHURCHILL

Knighted?!

BIGGE

Surely there is some law against it?

LADY CHURCHILL

The man's a common Indian, for God's sake.

MISS PHIPPS

And a Muslim.

ALICK YORKE

She can't just do what she likes.

DR REID

That's right. We are the ones who make this palace work
and we are being ignored and exploited. We have to stand
up to this wanton bullying.

BIGGE

Exactly. This is a usurpation of the basic tenets of
leadership.

ALICK YORKE

There are moral standards at stake. What is this? The Year
of the Munshi?

They all laugh.

LADY CHURCHILL

I propose we should rise up as a household and demand
that she retracts.

MISS PHIPPS

But she's the Queen.

LADY CHURCHILL

She is *our* sovereign. Her position is entirely based on the
implicit contract she makes with *us*. Who manages the
estates? Who is up at the crack of dawn preparing her
breakfast? Toadying to foreign diplomats? Eating those
interminable meals? Listening to the infernal drivel? Lords
and Ladies, the time has come to say no. We must stand
together and show her who really runs this ship.

PONSONBY

But this is a palace coup.

LADY CHURCHILL

It is an assertion of our inalienable rights as the aristocracy
of this country. The monarchy is not there by divine right.

PONSONBY

I think it is, actually.

LADY CHURCHILL

Oh shut up.

BIGGE

I agree. We must resist these foreign intruders, for the sake
of England, the Empire and St George.

LADY CHURCHILL

I say: either she drops this preposterous insult or we will
all leave.

GENERAL ASSENT

Hear, hear!

MISS PHIPPS

But isn't this treason?

LADY CHURCHILL

This is politics. The bloody unions do it. I don't see why we
shouldn't have a go.

Hooray!

ALICK YORKE

The Nabob has met his match.

Yes! Yes!

BIGGE

Let's show them what we are made of.

More approval!

That we are prepared to stand up to tyranny: for justice, for right and for England!

Huge cheers.

LADY CHURCHILL

Are you with me?

Unanimous assent.

Are you with me?

Unanimous assent and self-congratulation apart from:

ALICK YORKE

So what should we do?

Nobody is sure.

DR REID

Somebody has to tell her.

They all suddenly look nervous.

BIGGE

We should make a deputation.

ALICK YORKE

Won't that look like a cabal?

LADY CHURCHILL

I think you should go. You are the head of Household

PONSONBY

I couldn't possibly go, it would bring the position into disrepute.

ALICK YORKE
You know her quite well, Mrs Tuck.

MRS TUCK
I'm just a dresser. What about Miss Phipps?

Everyone's attention is drawn to the skinny, mild-mannered, nervous Lady in Waiting.

LADY CHURCHILL
Brilliant. You're the maid of honour. Exactly the person to break the news.

Miss Phipps looks terrified.

INT. COUNCIL CORRIDOR. OSBORNE HOUSE. NIGHT

Mrs Tuck fusses over Miss Phipps, making her look just so. Ponsonby, Dr Reid and Lady Churchill are there.

PONSONBY
Off you go – and don't take no for an answer.

The poor woman is terrified. She timidly makes her way up the stairs. She stops and looks back. Lady Churchill gives her a look of stern admonishment. Phipps nervously carries on. Then stops again. It's grandma's footsteps. Churchill ushers her on again.

INT. OUTSIDE THE COUNCIL ROOM. NIGHT

A terrified Miss Phipps knocks meekly on the double doors.

INT. QUEEN'S STUDY. NIGHT

Miss Phipps walks nervously across the vast room to the little table where Queen Victoria is sitting alone at her letters. The Queen looks up, clearly displeased to be interrupted. Miss Phipps is shaking. The Queen stares at her full of indignant expectation.

MISS PHIPPS
Erm . . .

QUEEN VICTORIA
Speak up.

Miss Phipps tries to gather herself and stop herself collapsing.

MISS PHIPPS

Your Majesty . . .

QUEEN VICTORIA

Out with it, girl, we are very busy.

MISS PHIPPS

There is something I must say that . . .

She looks at the Queen, terrified.

QUEEN VICTORIA

What is the meaning of this? Stop shaking.

MISS PHIPPS

I have come to ask you to reconsider the elevation of . . .
of Mr Karim.

The Queen can't quite believe her ears.

QUEEN VICTORIA

What did you say?

MISS PHIPPS

I have come to ask you not to give Mr Karim a knighthood,
Your Majesty.

QUEEN VICTORIA

Why the devil not?

MISS PHIPPS

The members of the Household demand that you abandon
your plans, Your Majesty.

QUEEN VICTORIA

Demand?!

MISS PHIPPS

We believe that it degrades the very concept of knighthood.
He comes from a very low family, Your Majesty. And he is
coloured.

QUEEN VICTORIA

Get out of my sight.

86

Miss Phipps looks like she's beginning to crack.

QUEEN VICTORIA
Did you not hear me?

MISS PHIPPS
Your Majesty, I must inform you that if you refuse – the entire Household will resign.

The Queen cannot believe her ears. She pauses for a moment. Then lets out an earth-shattering scream of rage:

QUEEN VICTORIA
Treason! Treason!

She sweeps the table in anger, evicting her Fabergé egg.

INT. KITCHENS, THE SAME

Miss Phipps is given whisky.

INT. OUTSIDE THE QUEEN'S STUDY, THE SAME

Ponsonby, Bertie and Reid approach the Queen's study.

INT. QUEEN'S STUDY. DAY

Bertie, Ponsonby and Reid march into the room. The Queen is sitting with Abdul. Abdul stands up and moves out of the way.

BERTIE
Mummy. Enough is enough. You are bringing the monarchy into crisis. And you are humiliating yourself for no good reason. You will drop this Munshi business forthwith. Do you hear me?

She stares at him.

The Munshi is a servant. He is an ignorant, pox-ridden, Indian peasant. Did you really think the Household would countenance such an insult?

QUEEN VICTORIA
I will not be disobeyed.

BERTIE

No, I've put up with you for over fifty years. You will drop this forthwith or . . .

QUEEN VICTORIA

Or? . . . Or? . . .

BERTIE

We will have you certified insane. And removed from office immediately. Here are the papers. Signed by Dr Reid.

The Queen is stunned. She looks at Dr Reid, who appears terrified of the whole situation.

QUEEN VICTORIA

I am eighty-one years of age. I have had nine children, forty-two grandchildren, and almost a billion citizens. I have rheumatism, a collapsed uterus, am morbidly obese, deaf in one ear. I have known eleven prime ministers, passed 2,347 pieces of legislation. I have been in office for sixty-two years, 234 days – thus I am the longest-serving monarch in world history. I am responsible for five households and a staff of more than three thousand. I am cantankerous, boring, greedy, ill-tempered, at times selfish and myopic, metaphorically and literally. I am, perhaps, disagreeably attached to power and should not have smashed the Emperor of Russia's egg. But I am anything but insane. If the Household wish to disobey me, so be it – let them do it face to face. I will see everyone in the Durbar Room. At once!

She marches out past Abdul:

Where on earth did you get gonorrhoea?

INT. OSBORNE HOUSE. DURBAR ROOM. DAY

The Durbar Room is full. The chief members of the Royal Household are there: Ponsonby, Reid, Phipps, Lady Churchill, but so are the pages, footmen and the maids. The Queen marches in to face them.

QUEEN VICTORIA

I understand there is some concern over my desires on preferment. I understand that feelings have run high and I understand that you have decided to resign rather than withstand my decision. If any one of you would like to tender their resignation it will be accepted without any unfortunate consequences – but at least have the decency to do it to my face. If anyone wishes to resign, please step forward.

She stares at them, absolutely formidable. Nervousness. People looking at one another. Small feints, but no one moves. Abdul is watching from the doorway.

QUEEN VICTORIA

I would like to inform you that I have decided against awarding any knighthoods at this moment.

Relief all round that she's come to her senses.

QUEEN VICTORIA

Instead, you will be delighted to know I have decided to make the Munshi a Commander of the Royal Victorian Order as a special token of my personal esteem for his services to the Empire. That will be all.

Ponsonby is so overcome he has to sit down. The Queen is shaking. She walks through the middle of the crowd who part to observe their customary obsequies. She walks out into the corridor.

INT. INDIAN CORRIDOR. OSBORNE HOUSE. DAY

The Queen walks out into the corridor alone. But we see she is faltering. Abdul sees her and runs the whole length of the corridor and catches her in his arms. Dr Reid and Mrs Tuck arrive. Reid pushes Abdul out of the way to get to the Queen.

DR REID

Satisfied?

Reid pushes Abdul away from the Queen. Then suddenly a shaken Ahmed arrives.

AHMED

Dr Reid! Dr Reid! It's Mr Mohammed!

EXT. GRAVEYARD. DAY

A devastated Abdul is at Mohammed's funeral. The Queen is with Abdul, Mrs Karim, the mother-in-law and Ahmed. Dr Reid and Ponsonby stand nearby out of duty to Her Majesty. Reid turns to Ponsonby.

DR REID

One down.

Abdul stands by the grave as the others leave.

ABDUL

I am sorry, my friend.

Then Abdul helps lead the Queen away.

QUEEN VICTORIA

We need to talk.

EXT. CARRIAGE. GROUNDS OF OSBORNE HOUSE. DAY

After the funeral. The Queen and Abdul sit in the open carriage. The Queen is wrapped up against the cold weather but looks very frail. She takes Abdul's hand.

QUEEN VICTORIA

I think it's time that you went home, Abdul.

ABDUL

This is my home.

QUEEN VICTORIA

I have been short-sighted and selfish. You are a young man, Abdul. Your whole life ahead of you.

ABDUL

But, Your Majesty –

QUEEN VICTORIA

I cannot protect you if I am not here. You must go, Abdul –

with your wife. The vultures are already circling. I don't even
think I will see this year out. All these stupid ceremonies.
What is the point in them, Abdul? They will kill me.

ABDUL

You will live for many more years, Your Majesty.

QUEEN VICTORIA

No. Abdul, I am sick and weary. I can hardly see, barely
hear. The Empress of half the world and I can't get in and
out of my own carriage.

ABDUL

I cannot leave you. I am your Munshi.

QUEEN VICTORIA

You must protect yourself. How could we have been so
blind? Forget me, Abdul. You have been a very good friend.

ABDUL

They can do what they like, but every day I will come and
be at your side as long as I shall live.

QUEEN VICTORIA

You are a silly fool, Abdul. But I adore you.

Snow falls all around them. Abdul holds the Queen's hand.

INT. CORRIDOR. OSBORNE HOUSE. DAY

The Queen, now ill, is wheeled along the corridor.

INT. THE SAME, QUEEN'S BEDCHAMBER

The Queen is now in bed unconscious, surrounded by the Household.

INT. CORRIDOR OUTSIDE QUEEN'S BEDCHAMBER. NIGHT

*Abdul is waiting outside the door. Ponsonby and Reid come out
looking grave.*

DR REID

I think you should inform the Kaiser.

EXT. OSBORNE HOUSE. NIGHT

Wide shot of the house at night. A light shining from an upstairs room.

INT. THE SAME, CORRIDOR

Abdul is dutifully standing sentry outside the Queen's room.

EXT. OSBORNE HOUSE. DAWN

Wide shot of Osborne House. Carriages arrive. The Kaiser gets out.

INT. CORRIDOR. THE SAME

The Kaiser et al. walk past Abdul into the Queen's room. The door is closed.

INT. QUEEN'S BEDCHAMBER. OSBORNE HOUSE. DAWN

The darkened room is full. On one side of the bed is the Kaiser, on the other is Bertie. They look at the Queen, who appears to be asleep. Suddenly she stirs. There is a gasp in the room. She opens her eyes. Dr Reid takes away the oxygen mask. Bertie takes her hand.

> QUEEN VICTORIA

Abdul?

> BERTIE

It's me, Mummy. And your grandson, Wilhelm. The Kaiser.

She takes the Kaiser's hand.

> QUEEN VICTORIA

No fighting when I'm gone. Promise me. Where is my Munshi?

> BERTIE

Hush. Hush. Everything is fine.

> QUEEN VICTORIA

But I need my Munshi. Where is the Munshi?

Bertie, hurt that he is not enough, gives in.

Bring her the Munshi.

INT. CORRIDOR OUTSIDE QUEEN'S BEDCHAMBER. DAY

Abdul is resolutely standing by.

DR REID

Don't you dare upset her.

INT. QUEEN'S BEDCHAMBER. OSBORNE HOUSE. DAY

The crowds of dignitaries part to let Abdul through. He approaches her sadly, and holds her hand.

QUEEN VICTORIA

Abdul?

ABDUL

Yes. I am here.

QUEEN VICTORIA

I want to talk to the Munshi alone.

DR REID

I think Your Majesty might . . .

QUEEN VICTORIA

I said: alone!

INT. CORRIDOR. THE SAME

The Kaiser, Bertie, the Household et al. all troop into the corridor.

INT. THE QUEEN'S BEDCHAMBER. THE SAME

The Queen has been propped up with pillows. Abdul kneels by her bedside. Dr Reid is discreetly at the back of the room, in the shadows. The Queen takes some oxygen then turns to Abdul.

QUEEN VICTORIA

When I was young I used to long for death. And now when

there is nothing to live for I cling on to life with every breath. I am scared, Abdul.

ABDUL

Don't be scared.

Abdul quotes a poem in Hindi. Then translates it:

QUEEN VICTORIA

'Listen, little drop, give up yourself without regret
And in exchange you will gain the ocean.
Give yourself away
And in the arms of the Great Sea be secure.'
The Great poet Rumi.

She squeezes Abdul's hand.

ABDUL

Prema puri hai. Hama kevala tukare kara rahe haim. 'Love is the whole. We are only pieces.'

QUEEN VICTORIA

That is very beautiful. You are a teacher, Abdul.

ABDUL

Everybody knows Rumi.
Allah is the teacher.
Love is the whole.
Prema puri hai.
We are only pieces.
Hama kevala tukare kara rahe haim.

QUEEN VICTORIA

'Prema puri hai. Hama kevala tukare kara rahe haim.'
Alhamdulilah!
I keep thinking I am falling.

ABDUL

Fall. Everything will be well. You are about to go to a much safer place.

QUEEN VICTORIA

To the Banquet Hall of Eternity.

ABDUL

Yes. Goodbye, my Queen.

Abdul is crying. The Queen holds on to Abdul's hand.

QUEEN VICTORIA

Goodbye. Take care, my sweet son.

She starts to nod off. Dr Reid puts his hand on Abdul's shoulder, clearly moved.

DR REID

Let her sleep.

INT. CORRIDOR

Abdul emerges still in tears. Bertie, the Kaiser, the Archbishop et al. all look on in pity as Abdul, completely absorbed, walks away. They troop back into the Queen's chamber.

INT. THE QUEEN'S BEDCHAMBER

Everyone has resumed their vigil. The junior serving girl yawns at the back. Suddenly we realise the Queen's oxygen bottle stops emitting bubbles. Bertie has the Queen's hand. He realises she has died.

INT. CORRIDOR OUTSIDE QUEEN'S BEDCHAMBER

Abdul is waiting outside. The doors open. Bertie appears. He looks Abdul in the eye with contempt.

EXT. PALACE GATES. OSBORNE HOUSE. DAY

Bigge, dressed immaculately in black with a top hat, walks to the gates to make an announcement.

BIGGE

I grieve to say Her Majesty passed away at half past six precisely. Long live the King.

INT. QUEEN'S STUDY. OSBORNE HOUSE. DAY

Bertie in the darkness of the Queen's study. He throws open the shutters himself, morning light floods in. He sits at the Queen's desk – it's his now.

INT. QUEEN'S BEDCHAMBER. OSBORNE HOUSE. DAY

Mrs Tuck throws open the curtains as she did at the beginning of the film. The crepuscular room is flooded with light. Maids throw off the sheets. The Queen's body is blanched.

INT. QUEEN'S STUDY. OSBORNE HOUSE. DAY

Bertie looks down and sees on the desk her Urdu journals.

INT. CORRIDOR OUTSIDE QUEEN'S BEDCHAMBER

Mrs Tuck comes out of the Queen's bedchamber. She takes Abdul's hand and leads him into the room.

INT. QUEEN'S BEDCHAMBER

The Queen has been transformed into a transcendental vision. We see Abdul transfixed by the dead Queen. Slowly, with great reverence, he kneels before her.

ABDUL

May Allah bless you.

He kisses her feet. Finally as he raises his head we see his devastated sadness. Then his look turns from one of devastated loss to one of foreboding.

INT. CORRIDOR, OSBORNE HOUSE

Abdul walks out along the corridor and down the grand staircase. On the sound track we hear the sound of violent banging on a door.

VOICE
(out of shot)
Open up in the name of the King!

EXT. ABDUL'S COTTAGE. DAY

Mrs Karim opens the front door. Suddenly several henchmen appear pushing her aside as they rush into the house.

INT. FRONT ROOM, ABDUL'S COTTAGE. DAY

The henchmen run into the room and start ransaking the place. Mrs Karim and her mother in full burqa try to prevent them taking things. A henchman goes past with a drawer stuffed with letters.

EXT. GARDEN, ABDUL'S COTTAGE. DAY

The henchmen have made a big pyre of the letters. One henchman pours petrol on and the whole thing goes up in flames. Bertie looks on contentedly, smoking a cigar. Mrs Karim runs out.

EXT. ROAD TO ABDUL'S COTTAGE. DAY

Abdul walking. He looks up to see smoke. He hears Mrs Karim scream and he starts to run.

EXT. GARDEN, ABDUL'S COTTAGE. DAY

A henchman throws on more letters. Mrs Karim, screaming, is now being restrained by a henchman. Suddenly there is a shout. Abdul comes running into the garden.

ABDUL

No!

Footmen hold back the screaming Abdul as the pyre burns.

BERTIE

I want you out of here immediately.

Satisfied, he leaves. Mrs Karim takes Abdul's hand.

MRS KARIM

They've taken everything.

She surreptitiously gives him something as the pyre burns. He looks down. She has given him the locket. He holds it tight. The smoke of the fire obscures everything.

INT. PASSENGER FERRY, SOLENT. MISTY MORNING

The smoke turns into mist on the Solent. We are on a ferry. Abdul and his wife as it pulls away from shore. No one recognises Abdul. He opens his palm to reveal the Queen's locket. Looking back, he disappears into the mist as the boat sails away.

INT. DARKENED ROOM, AGRA. MORNING

As in the beginning of the film, shutters are opened on to bright daylight as a muezzin calls to prayers.

EXT. ROOFTOP, AGRA

As before, we see a figure from behind praying. The rooftops of Agra below, the Taj Mahal in the distance.

Title:

ABDUL RETURNED TO AGRA IN 1901

EXT. STREETS, AGRA. BRIGHT DAY

The bustle of an Agra street. A figure makes his way through the chaotic street life as in the opening of the film. But this time the figure is slow. We follow him from behind and see he has grey hair. We realise this is Abdul. He makes his way determinedly through the city to a park.

EXT. AGRA, PARK

Abdul makes his way to a statue of Queen Victoria. He kneels. We think he is praying but he kisses the Queen's feet.

ABDUL
Good morning, Your Majesty.

Abdul sits on the base of the statue. He looks out at the crowds passing by. In his hand we see the locket – the camera slowly cranes back. Abdul the faithful retainer has kept his word: he remains loyally with his Queen despite everything.

Title:

HE DIED NINE YEARS LATER

We crane above the statue to see the whole vista of Agra. The Taj Mahal glistening in the background.

Title:

INDIA GAINED INDEPENDENCE IN 1947

The End.

CHAPTER 1

VIENNA, AUSTRIA

I was born in Vienna, Austria on August 28, 1927. Although my parents named me Avraham Abba, the government also assigned me the German name of "Adolf." My father, Chaim Perlmutter, and my mother, Malka Perlmutter (née Gottlieb), were born near Lvov in Galicia, then part of the Austro-Hungarian Empire. My father was drafted into the Austrian army during World War I, became a prisoner-of-war on the Russian front and was released at the end of the war in 1918. Shortly after, Galicia became part of Poland, and many Jews, including both of my parents and their families, moved to Vienna.

My parents married in Vienna on June 3, 1923. They made a modest living, working hard in their small textile store on the Grosse Sperlgasse in the 2nd Bezirk (District). We lived in a small ground-floor, four-room apartment on the Nestroygasse #5. By modern standards, our living conditions were primitive. My father's mother, Rachel Perlmutter (née Teichberg), occupied one bedroom and kitchen until her death in 1936. My parents, my sister Dorothea (Thea, born August 6, 1924), and I lived in the remaining rooms, also a bedroom and kitchen. Two water closets lay at the end of the hall outside our apartment: one for us and one for our next-door neighbors. Our kitchen featured running water, but we had no shower or bathtub. Our mother washed the laundry in a wooden trough, which she also used to bathe my sister and me when we were babies. When we outgrew this, we used a large bowl to wash ourselves.

My parents came from Orthodox Jewish families and reared us in the same manner. One of the apartments on the first floor had been converted to a synagogue, and my father and I prayed there every day. Every Thursday evening my mother cooked for the Sabbath and baked *challahs*, twisted leavened bread.

3

The Gottlieb family, 1920
From left to right: Iro, Grandma Frima (née Feldberg), Malka, Beile Perl (Peppi), Chancie
(Anni), Grandpa Moses (not shown: Ze'ev)

Avraham's parents, Malka and Chaim Perlmutter, on their wedding day, June 3, 1923

Avraham (Av) in front of his childhood apartment on the Nestroygasse #5 in Vienna, 2003

The textile store of Av's parents on the Grosse Sperlgasse in Vienna, 1990

I was a wild child. Even at the age of two, my adventurous spirit—which would serve me so well years later—was evident. At that time, a young woman watched over me until my mother came home from the store. I often climbed on a chair in front of a bedroom window facing the street so I could watch the neighborhood kids playing soccer and an occasional horse-drawn carriage passing by. I yearned to get out into the street, but was too small to reach the front-door handle. One day, I threw a ball out the window and asked our nanny to let me out to retrieve it. Once outside, I dashed several blocks to the Danube Canal. A policeman found me standing by a round advertising kiosk by the side of the canal and took me to a nearby police station. Since I was unable to provide my full name or address, he kept me at the station until my distraught mother arrived to notify them of my disappearance. She was relieved to find me there in good health.

I began my formal education at the age of six, attending a nearby Hebrew school on the Malzgasse. I was often a class troublemaker, and as punishment the teacher made me stand in a corner in the front of the room. On one such occasion toward the end of the school year, I slowly moved from one corner to another while the teacher faced the class. Most of the other children watched me in amusement, ignoring the lesson. When the instructor realized I had moved, he sentenced me to the most severe punishment. Taking a small bamboo cane from his desk drawer, he ordered me to hold out both hands. He attempted several times to hit me, but each time he struck I pulled my hands aside to avoid the cane. This earned me a visit to the school principal, who admonished me. At the end of the day, I snuck back into the empty classroom, went to the teacher's desk drawer, and broke the cane in half. Soon after, the school informed my parents that I would not be permitted to return the next school year.

For the next three years I went to an elementary school on the Kleine Pfarrgasse, across the street from a Catholic church. I was one of maybe three Jewish boys in a class of 30 students, and enjoyed my relationship with the other students. We often wrestled with each other one-against-one, and the others admired me for being among the strongest.

I continued my religious education by attending a daily one-hour class taught by my uncle, Rabbi Dr. Wolf (Ze'ev) Gottlieb, in an apartment located on the Taborstrasse. All the students sat at a large table and my uncle made me sit next to him. Quite often, I was so unruly in the class that he slapped me.

After school, I often played soccer in the street with other neighborhood boys. I also loved to jump on the back of horse-drawn carriages when they passed by on our street. Occasionally I went to the small restaurant operated by my relative Moshe Eilen, who taught me the basics of chess. Once, in my first attempt to pursue the "study of aerodynamics," I climbed on top of a high piece of furniture and jumped down using an open umbrella as a "parachute." The umbrella turned inside-out, and I was fortunate to get away with only a few bruises as I crashed to the floor.

My peaceful childhood changed dramatically on March 13, 1938, when, in the Nazi-controlled Reichstag, Hitler announced the Anschluss (union) with Austria. Two days later, I witnessed Hitler as he entered Vienna, standing in a moving car with his right hand outstretched in the Nazi salute, during a parade on the Praterstrasse. Immediately after the Anschluss, the Nazis began a brutal crackdown on Austrian Jews, arresting and publicly humiliating them. I was terrified when I saw Austrian Nazis and other local residents stand by and watch as German soldiers forced Jews to get down on their hands and knees and scrub the pavement with toothbrushes. My erstwhile class friends also reacted to the anti-Semitic propaganda by ganging up on me and beating me severely. I no longer dared to attend classes for the balance of my fourth school year.

On May 18, 1938, my concerned parents submitted a questionnaire to the Emigration Department of the Assistance Center of the Israelite Culture Organization to request permission for our family to leave Austria (see Appendix C for related documents). Most countries, however, refused to admit Jewish refugees. While my parents tried to get visas to immigrate to Trinidad, a country that allowed Jewish immigration during the 1930s, I read excitedly in an encyclopedia about the many wild animals living on that remote island. Unfortunately, around that time Trinidad instituted new immigration restrictions and the request was denied.

Thea and Av, 1932

Av's uncle Rabbi Ze'ev Gottlieb and his wife, Betty (the daughter of the Chief Rabbi of Romania), 1939. After being detained by the Gestapo during the war, Rabbi Ze'ev was released and then fled to England with his wife. He later became the Chief Rabbi of Scotland, before retiring in Israel. They have two daughters, Dr. Avivah Gottlieb Zornberg and Dr. Freema Gottlieb (both renowned authors).

Av, 1938

In September 1938, I enrolled in a gymnasium (middle school) for Jewish students only, located on the Kleine Sperlgasse. For a few months I enjoyed studying many interesting subjects, including algebra, geometry and Latin.

But the terror of the outside world was closing in fast. I clearly remember the night of November 9, 1938, when the Nazis took to the streets of Germany and Austria, attacked and murdered Jews, broke into synagogues and private houses, and destroyed and burned Torah scrolls. The Nazis called that night *Kristallnacht* ("Crystal Night") because of the millions of pieces of glass that remained after the destruction.

On that single night, hundreds of Jews were killed, thousands were injured or arrested and deported to concentration camps, and 1,574 synagogues were burned or destroyed. The violence was particularly brutal in Vienna, where 6,000 Jews were arrested and deported to concentration camps and almost all of the city's synagogues were destroyed. German and Austrian police and firefighters who witnessed the destruction were silent and did not intervene. As I found out later, the world observed from outside and did almost nothing.

9

On that night, my parents stayed at home and asked me to check whether their store was damaged. As I proceeded along the Leopoldstrasse I saw a frenzied mob entering and destroying the Polish Synagogue, which my family occasionally attended. I also watched several Nazis force two elderly Jewish men to the ground and order them to use toothbrushes to clean graffiti on the sidewalk. In the meantime, my mother begged our Christian neighbor, Mrs. Kauer, to look for me and bring me home.

During that time, my father and my uncle Rabbi Ze'ev Gottlieb went to hide in a neighbor's apartment across the street. When my sister no longer detected any Nazis on our street, she went to my father and uncle and told them it appeared to be safe to return home. Just when they crossed the street, several Nazis arrived and started beating my father and uncle. My sister screamed at the soldiers to stop, and the Nazis allowed them to return to our house.

My parents began to desperately search for other ways for us to leave Austria. Because my mother's sister Anni Bachrach and her family lived in the Netherlands, my parents decided they would attempt to send my sister and me there with the *Kindertransport*—a refugee children's transport operation that enabled Jewish children under the age of seventeen from Germany, Austria, Czechoslovakia and Poland to flee Nazi-controlled countries on temporary travel documents to the United Kingdom, Belgium, or the Netherlands. Most of the approximately 10,000 children were transported to the United Kingdom, but almost 2,000 children were sent to the Netherlands between November 1938 and September 1939.

On November 21, 1938, my aunt Anni sent the Dutch government a request that I, my 14-year old sister, Thea; my ten-year-old cousin, Herbert Fink; my nine-year-old cousin, Renée Fink (the children of my mother's sister Peppi Fink and her husband Jacob); and my cousin Channa (Hanni) join her in the Netherlands. This request was granted. About the same time, my uncle Rabbi Ze'ev Gottlieb arranged for Thea, Herbert, Renée, and me to be included on the list of children that would travel on the Kindertransport from Vienna to the Netherlands. Hanni left Vienna with her parents at a later time.

Den Haag, 21 November 1938.   5072

Weled. Hooggeb. Vrouwe,

A, B, C.

    Naar aanleiding van het telefonisch onderhoud, dat ik heden de eer had met U te mogen hebben deel ik U by dezen de namen van de kinderen mee wel ik gaarne in ons Vaderland had ondergebracht.

    Het betreft hier het byna 4 jarig dochtertje van myn broer, genaamd Hanni Gottlieb, wonende te Weenen XX Traisengasse 16/27. Myn broer is met zyn gezin uitgewezen en moet de volgende maand het land verlaten hebben. Hy is echter in het bezit van een affidavit voor Amerika.

    Herbart en René= Fink een jongen en een meisje, respectievelyk 10 en 9 jaar, wonende te Weenen X, Hertzgasse 13/13 hun ouders myn zuster en zwager wenschen te emigreeren maar Australie,

    Thea en Adolf Perlmutter een maxi meisje en jongen respectievelyk 14 en 12 jaar, wonende te Weenen II, Nestroygasse 5 /2 hun ouders myn zuster en zwager wenschen te emigreeren naar Australie , landingsgeld voor hen is gestort.

    Ik zelf ben door huwelyk Nederlandsche en heb een uitgebreide Nederlandsche familie, waar ik de kinderen met genoegen kan onderbrengen . Wenscht gy echter de kinderen niet by myn familie ondergebracht, doch in een gemeenschappelyk tehuis, dan ga ik ook hier mee accoord, hoewel ik aan huisvesting by myn familie de voorkeur geef.

    Myn man ix alsmede de heeren J. Huisman vander Duynstraat 11 H alhier en S. Poons Molenstraat alhier zullen voor de kinderen garant zyn.

    Aangezien het onderbrengen hier van deze kinderen aan de emigratie der ouders zeer ter stade zal komen, zal het door my zeer worden gewaardeerd, indien U kunt bewerkstelligen, dat deze arme kinderen - die reeds zoo langen tyd de ellende aan den lyve hebben gevoeld - spoedig naar Nederland mogen komen.

                          Hoogacht end,
                          Uw dw. drs.

A. Bachrach - Gottlieb
Weteringkade 27

Request (in Dutch) from Av's aunt Anni Bachrach to the Dutch government that Av (listed as Adolf), Thea, and his three cousins join her in the Netherlands. (National Archives, The Hague, Zorg voor de vluchtelingen uit Duitsland, 1938-1942, 2.04.58, inv. nr. 113)

On January 11, 1939, our parents brought us to the railroad station. I was wearing a suit—the best clothes I owned at the time—and carried with me a valise containing additional clothes, family photos, and sandwiches my parents had packed for us. My mother spoke with a cry in her voice, begging my sister, who was three years older than I, to watch over me in the Netherlands. As the train started leaving the station, I waved to my anguished parents.

That was the last time I saw my mother.

Thea; Av's mother, Malka; and Av, December 1938

CHAPTER 2

REFUGEE CAMPS IN THE NETHERLANDS

The train, with several hundred Jewish children aboard, made very few stops as it traveled west through the beautiful countryside of Austria and Southern Germany. While looking out of the windows, most of the children were sad, having been separated from their parents, and worried about their future. Some of the smaller children wept with anguish as the older ones tried to comfort them. I was somewhat relieved that I was traveling with my sister, and to a country where our aunt Anni Bachrach had been living since she arrived as a refugee during World War I. She and her husband, Abraham (Aby) Bachrach, lived on 27 Weteringskade in Den Haag ('s-Gravenhage) with their two children, Hyman and Thea Henrietta (in 1942, they had a third child, Klara).

In the early evening, many hours after we left Vienna, we arrived at the German-Dutch border. The train stopped and a number of German policemen boarded and walked through the cars, checking that no adults had smuggled themselves inside. We waited anxiously for the train to resume its journey, and we cheered when it soon stopped again and Dutch policemen entered the cars. We knew that finally we were safe.

Several hours later, we arrived at our destination, Emmahuis, in Wijk aan Zee, a small town on the North Sea coast, west of Amsterdam. As we stepped down from the train cars, several nuns welcomed us in broken German and told us that soon we would each be treated to a good meal and a bed to sleep on in their campsite barracks. This Catholic summer camp was given the task of providing a temporary home for Jewish refugee children. The nuns were wonderfully kind and treated us with great respect, and they encouraged us to say our Jewish prayers

13

Some of the boys who arrived with Av and Thea in Wijk aan Zee, January 1939. Av is third from the left in the front row. In the center of the back row are two of the wonderful nuns who took care of the children

Another photo of Av in Wijk aan Zee, January 1939. Av is in the center of the front row (Collection Jewish Historical Museum, Amsterdam)

14

before and after each meal. Every morning they took us for a long walk along the dunes outside the camp, and urged us to rest in our beds for one hour after each midday meal.

In March 1939, after about two months in Wijk aan Zee, many of the children, including Thea and me, were transferred to Ons Boschhuis, a refugee camp in the town of Driebergen (about 50 miles southeast). The camp officials provided us with paper, envelopes, and stamps and encouraged us to write to our parents. I joined the camp's soccer team, which played a number of matches against other youth teams in the city. I was overjoyed to once again be able to participate in my favorite sport. I also started to read my first book in Dutch, an American Western cowboy story. I tried to understand the meaning of each sentence by reading it repeatedly, searching for words that were similar to German. Slowly but surely I learned the meaning of an increasing number of Dutch words, and enjoyed reading the adventures in the story.

My aunt Anni and her husband, Aby, came to visit and told us they were trying to arrange for our release from the camp so we could live with them. However, this was a laborious process that would take many months. Several weeks thereafter, a number of children, including Thea and me, were transferred to another refugee camp, Onze Bliscap, located several miles away in the city of Amerongen. I was very unhappy about this transfer until I was promised that transportation arrangements would be made so I could participate in every soccer game of the Driebergen team. The Amerongen camp was located in a forested area, and we enjoyed roaming the forest and picking blackberries.

Several weeks later, on June 29, 1939, Thea and I were again transferred, this time to a refugee camp located about 40 miles to the west in Gouda, a city famous for the cheese of the same name. This camp, Gouda Burgerweeshuis, was in the city center and we were not permitted to leave the grounds. The place had a number of ping-pong tables and I quickly learned and improved my game.

Thea and Av with the North Sea as a background, January 1939

Soccer team at the Ons Boschhuis refugee camp in Driebergen, 1939. Av is in the front row, third from the left (from the private collection of Hajo Meijer)

Three weeks after my arrival, I was infected by the diphtheria virus and transferred to a local hospital for observation. Fortunately, I did not experience any fever and was transferred to the quarantine camp Zeeburgerdijk in Amsterdam. In December 1939, I was found to be free of the virus and released into the custody of the Van Straten family, relatives of my aunt Anni, in Den Haag. I finally was able to again enjoy family life and have the opportunity to continue my education. During that time, Thea was transferred to a Youth Aliyah (Palestine Pioneer) camp in Loosdrecht, a small farming town east of Amsterdam, where children in their mid-to-late teens were trained for their planned immigration to Palestine.

Den Haag, 1 Mei 1939.

Het Departement van Binnenlandsche Zaken
Afdeeling Vluchtelingen
den Weled. Geb. Heer Buker(
te 's-Gravenhage

Weled. Geb. Heer,

By myn bezoek te departemente werd my tot myn groote teleurstelling medegedeeld, dat myn verzoek tot het in myn gezin opnemen van het kind Adolf Perlmutter uit Weenen, is afgewezen op grond van het feit, dat myn schoonvader, die lydende is aan T.B.C. te gelegentyd wel eens by my eet.

Het is my niet duidelyk, dat dit laatste zoo doorslaggevend is, daardoor het geluk van het bedoelde kind moet worden verstoord .

Immers het is slechts 1 x in de drie weken op Vrydagavond, dat myn schoonvader by my eet, terwyl wy bovendien met het oog op myn eigen kleine kinderen zeer strenge voorzorgsmaatregelen getroffen hebben, te weten eet myn schoonvader uit speciaal voor hem bestemde borden, gebruikt hy aparte lepels en vorken en drikt hy uit eigen kop en glas . Ook heeft hy aan tafel een speciale plaats verwyderd van de kinderen , terwyl het laken, waarmee de tafel tydens het eten is gedekt terstond na den maaltyd ter wassching wordt gegeven.

Als gy dit alles overweegt, dan zult gy wel begrypen dat wy niet lichtzinnig op dit gebied zyn en zal het U duidelyk zyn ,dat wy besmetting voor onze kleine kinderen 1 en 3 jaar hebben weten te vermyden, wy hiertoe met hulp van het Allerhoogste Wezen zeer zeker voor een grooter kind (11 jaar) instaat zullen zyn.

Inmiddels heb ik deze kwestie met myn schoonvader besproken en terstond gaf hy my te kennen het geluk van den jongeling niet in den weg te willen staan, mitsdien hy zich bereid verklaarde by my nimmer meer den maaltyd te gebruiken.

Nu de zaak dus gewyzigd is en eenig bezwaar van medische zyde niet meer aanwezig is zou ik U willen verzoeken het besluit te doen herzien en alsnog de toestemming te willen verleenen.

Ik wys U er speciaal op, dat dit laatste geen holle fraze is en ik bereid ben er een schriftelyke verklaring voor af te leggen.

Ook ben ik bereid indien gewenscht een attest van den geneesheer myner kinderen, arts Simons (kinder-arts) ,die myn kinderen onder voortdurende controle heeft by U over te leggen.

In het byzonder wil ik nog Uw aandacht vragen voor het feit, dat Adolf Perlmutter uit zeer streng orthodoxe huize komt, zoodat het hoogstnoodzakelyk is, dat thans eindelyk weer eens begonnen wordt met zyn religieuze vorming, waartoe in myn gezin alleszins gelegenheid bestaat.

Gaarne wil ik U een en ander nog eens mondeling toelichten en verzoek ik U beleefd my daartoe dezer dagen gelegenheid te geven.

Uw gunstig antwoord zie ik dan ook gaarne tegemoet.

A. Bachrach-Gottlieb Wateringkade 27.

Hoogachtend,

Av's aunt Anni's request (in Dutch) to the Department of Internal Affairs Refugees Division in Den Haag on May 1, 1939, where she asks that Av be allowed to leave the refugee camp to live with her. She stresses that Av is strictly Orthodox and it is important he have a religious education. (National Archives, The Hague, Zorg voor de vluchtelingen uit Duitsland, 1938-1942, 2.04.58, inv. nr. 120)

18

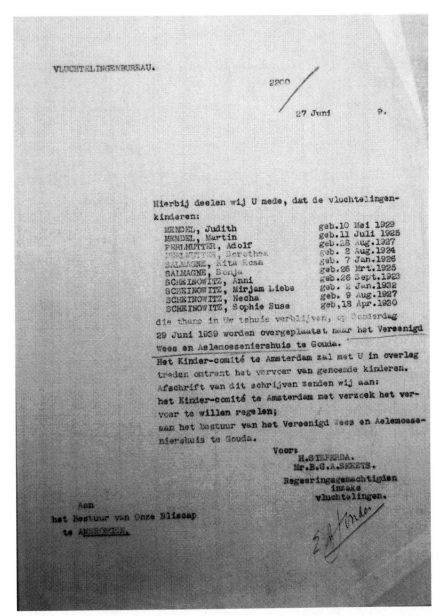

VLUCHTELINGENBUREAU.

2200

27 Juni   9.

Hierbij deelen wij U mede, dat de vluchtelingen-
kinderen:

MENDEL, Judith	geb.10 Mei 1929
MENDEL, Martin	geb.11 Juli 1925
PERLMUTTER, Adolf	geb.28 Aug.1927
PERLMUTTER, Dorothea	geb. 2 Aug.1924
SALMAGNE, Rita Rosa	geb. 7 Jan.1926
SALMAGNE, Sonja	geb.26 Mrt.1925
SCHEINOWITZ, Anni	geb.26 Sept.1923
SCHEINOWITZ, Mirjam Liebe	geb. 2 Jan.1932
SCHEINOWITZ, Necha	geb. 9 Aug.1927
SCHEINOWITZ, Sophie Suse	geb.18 Apr.1930

die thans in Uw tehuis verblijven, op Donderdag
29 Juni 1939 worden overgeplaatst naar het Vereenigd
Wees en Aelemoeseniershuis te Gouda.
Het Kinder-comité te Amsterdam zal met U in overleg
treden omtrent het vervoer van genoemde kinderen.
Afschrift van dit schrijven zenden wij aan:
het Kinder-comité te Amsterdam met verzoek het vervoer te willen regelen;
aan het bestuur van het Vereenigd Wees en Aelemoeseniershuis te Gouda.

Voor:
H.SIKKERDA.
Mr.B.G.A.SMEETS.
Regeeringsgemachtigden
inzake
vluchtelingen.

Aan
het Bestuur van Onze Blijdschap
te AMERONGEN.

*Letter to the Boards of the Amerongen and Gouda refugee camps listing the children,
including Av and Thea (third and fourth names listed), to be transferred on June 29, 1939
(National Archives, The Hague, Zorg voor de vluchtelingen uit Duitsland, 1938-1942,
2.04.58, inv. nr. 126)*

19

MINISTERIE VAN BINNENLANDSCHE ZAKEN.

NR.

AFDEELING:
Vluchtelingenbureau.

'S-GRAVENHAGE, 8 December 1939.

BETREFFENDE:
Opname in gezinnen van
vluchtelingen-kinderen.

Men gelieve bij het antwoord nauwkeurig
het onderwerp, de dagteekening en het
nummer van dit schrijven te vermelden.

Hierbij deel ik U mede, dat krachtens machtiging van
Zijne Excellentie den Minister van Binnenlandsche Zaken de
vluchteling(e)

Adolf Perlmutter,   geb. 23-8-27

die thans in het Burgerweeshuis
verblijft, daaruit op 14 December 1939 zal worden ontslagen,
ten einde te worden opgenomen in het gezin van:

J. Straten, Soendastraat 42, 's Gravenhage

onder garantie van Uw Comité.

Ik verzoek U genoemd gezin tijdig met deze beslis-
sing in kennis te willen stellen en voor de uitvoering te
willen zorg dragen.

Voor   Mr. SIEPERDA,
Regeeringsgemachtigde
inzake vluchtelingen.

Het Hoofd Afdeeling ARMWEZEN,

Aan het Comité voor
Bijzondere Joodsche Belangen,
Lijnbaansgracht 366, Amsterdam C.

Afschrift van dit schrijven is toegezonden aan:
Het Kinder-Comité;
den Leider of het Bestuur van het Tehuis, waar het kind verblijft;
het Hoofd van de Politie ter plaatse van dit tehuis;
het Hoofd van de Politie ter plaatse, waar het gezin woont;
de Inspectie van de Bevolkingsregisters.
het pleeggezin.

4020 - '39

*Letter (in Dutch) from the Department of Internal Affairs in which Av is granted
permission to be placed with the Van Straten family in Den Haag in December 1939
(National Archives, The Hague, Zorg voor de vluchtelingen uit Duitsland, 1938-1942,
2.04.58, inv. nr. 120)*

CHAPTER 3

DEN HAAG

My aunt Anni, uncle Aby, and their two small children already were providing a home for my aunt Berta and uncle Iro Gottlieb, their daughter, Channa (Hanni), and my great-grandmother Feiga Feldberg, all of whom also managed to leave Austria. Accordingly, they asked Sientje, the sister of my uncle Aby, and her husband, Joop (Joseph) Van Straten, to take me, a 12-year-old stranger, into their household. Both were in their early thirties and had two small children, a boy named Hijman and a girl named Clara. They lived in a three-bedroom apartment in the Scheldestraat, a few blocks from my aunt.

I was given a bedroom with a window facing the street. I enrolled in the fifth grade at an elementary school within walking distance of my new home. I was pleased to find my cousin Herbert Fink in the same class. He and his sister, Renée, had come with us to the Netherlands in the Kindertransport and had found a home with other wonderful people.

My Dutch improved rapidly and I greatly enjoyed the teaching system used in the class. Our teacher gave us one point for each correctly solved homework mathematics problem. We could also earn points during class by correctly answering questions on geography and other subjects. Every Friday, the teacher added up the points earned by each student and assigned seats in accordance with the scores. The student with the most points was seated in the far-left seat in the last row in the back of the class, and the student with the least points on the far-right seat in the first row. Herbert and I generally competed with each other for the top points earned.

After school I often played soccer in the street with other neighborhood kids. One day, a local children's soccer coach recruited me for his team. I was thrilled to become one of the team's outstanding players. I also continued my high-risk adventures, dispensing with fear (and common sense) to climb up the outside walls of our two-story apartment building by clinging to the bricks with only my fingers and toes.

In the Netherlands, parents are traditionally strict disciplinarians. Hence at home, I was instructed to go to sleep at 8 PM, and Uncle Joop made sure the door to my bedroom was closed, the window shade pulled down, and the ceiling light turned off. I loved to read, however, so I attached a thin rope to the bottom of the shade, and from my bed managed to pull the shade sufficiently open to get enough light to read. Whenever I heard someone approaching the bedroom door, I released the rope to close the shade, and hid the book under my pillow.

My uncle Aby ensured I was properly trained in Jewish studies. Several days a week I went to his apartment and he taught me sections of the Torah (the Hebrew Bible) and explanations thereof as written by Hebrew scholars over the ages. Every Saturday morning I accompanied him for prayers in a local synagogue. In the month before the holidays of the Jewish New Year and Yom Kippur, we went to the synagogue each day before dawn. My uncle also arranged for me to have my Bar Mitzvah at the synagogue and a get-together with our close relatives afterward.

Life followed a normal routine until May 10, 1940, when the German Army invaded the Netherlands. Despite the Dutch military's brave efforts, the Germans were victorious after five days of fighting. After the bombing of Rotterdam, the Dutch surrendered. During those five days, the Jews who lived in the Netherlands, and especially the persecuted individuals who had fled there for safety, were shocked and horrified. Many tried to leave the country but these desperate attempts were generally unsuccessful. Uncle Joop thought it might be possible to arrange for my immigration to England. When I asked whether he and his family would join me, he said they would remain—he believed the Nazis would not dare hurt Dutch Jews. I told him I would not leave without them.

22

Aunt Anni Bachrach and son Hyman, 1936

Class photo, the Jewish Lyceum on Fisher Street in Den Haag, Fall 1941. Av is in the front row, second from the left (Collection Jewish Historical Museum, Amsterdam)

The Germans considered the Dutch fellow Aryans and the transition to Nazi rule in the Netherlands proceeded gradually. The atrocities experienced by the Jews of Vienna and other Austrian cities following the Nazi invasion did not immediately occur upon implementation of the German civil administration in the Netherlands. Instead, the Germans slowly instituted new laws restricting Jewish liberties. Dutch Jews were prohibited from serving as volunteer air-raid wardens and then dismissed from civil service and universities. By the end of 1940, all Jewish businesses had to be registered. By the beginning of 1941, the registration of all Jews living in the Netherlands began. Maps of each town identified the name, age, gender, marital status, and location of all resident Jews. I was included in that registration. On February 22, the Nazis commenced mass round-ups and arrests of Jews in Amsterdam.

Over the next two years, conditions in the Netherlands deteriorated for Jews. In January 1942, the concentration and expulsion of Jews began. All non-Dutch Jews were ordered to leave the coastal areas and relocate to Amsterdam. In May 1942, all Jews were required to permanently wear a Yellow Star of David with the word *Jood* (Jew) on the left chest area. By mid-July 1942, Jews were being deported to the Auschwitz concentration camp.

By the fall of 1942, I was ordered to leave Den Haag. That was the last time I saw or had contact with any of my relatives in Den Haag.

CHAPTER 4

AMSTERDAM

On October 7, 1942, I arrived in Amsterdam. I was sent to live in the Jewish Quarter with a widow named Suzanne Cohen (née Branden) and her two adult sons. Not only were the Cohens kind enough to provide me with a temporary home, they also treated me like a member of their family. I was assigned my own bedroom, and shortly after my arrival I enrolled in the first grade of a middle school a couple blocks away.

Life was relatively normal for some time. Once, I awoke in the morning with my face covered in snow that had drifted into the room through a partially opened window. On another occasion, I asked one of the Cohen sons if he would give me one of his cigarettes to smoke. He agreed on the condition that I had to inhale. After several inhalations I felt miserable and threw the cigarette away. That was the last time I touched a cigarette for many years.

Several months after my arrival in Amsterdam, I could no longer attend school because all Jewish schools were forced to close. This ended my formal education.

In the meantime we became aware that the German occupation forces, assisted by the Dutch police, were arresting Jews daily. Once arrested, the Jews were brought to, and concentrated in, a local theater before they were transported to "labor" camps in Poland. This theater, the Hollandsche Schouwburg, was renamed the Joodsche Schouwburg (the Jewish Theater) in October 1941. During 1942 and 1943, it was used as a deportation center for the Jews. Between 60,000 and 80,000 men, women, and children were deported from the theater, first to either the Westerbork or Vught transit camps, and from there to concentration camps at Auschwitz, Bergen-Belsen, or Sobibor. Unaware that these

25

so-called camps were extermination camps, the detainees rarely put up any resistance.

One evening, in March 1943, a police van stopped in front of the Cohen house. Several officers burst in and stormed past me into the living room shouting, "Where is Adolf Perlmutter?" They apparently thought they were there to arrest an adult, and ignoring me, climbed the stairs. In a bedroom they found one of the Cohen sons, who must have revealed my identity. The officers ordered both of us outside and into the rear of the van. They drove several blocks before stopping to arrest another Jewish man. Before entering the van, that man proposed a boxing match with two of the policemen. He suggested that if they won, he would go with them peacefully, and if he won, they would release him. The policemen instead shoved him into the rear of the van and transported all of us to the Jewish Theater.

Inside the theater, I observed hundreds of men and women sitting, quiet and resigned, on benches. I was one of only a few detainees who ate the offered sandwiches. Restless, I walked around and discovered that two armed German soldiers were guarding each exit. I noticed one particular pair left an exit unguarded while they retrieved their replacements. I suggested to the Cohen son that a temporarily unguarded exit might be an opportunity to escape. He told me he would not dare to do so since he feared the Germans would kill him if he were caught. I dropped the subject, but decided if the chance arose again, I would try to escape.

The Germans had arranged for an organization representing Jews—the "Joodse Raad"—to review with them the detainees' cases, but I believe that few, if any, Jews were saved from deportation. I did not wait for such a useless review. In the middle of the night when I saw that the soldiers again left an exit unguarded, I calmly walked out the unlocked door. Once outside, I ran the half mile back to the Cohen house and knocked on the door. When I told Mrs. Cohen of my escape, the poor woman, crying, asked me why her son was not with me. I explained his decision not to escape. (I learned many years later that he died in 1943 in either Auschwitz or Sobibor, and Mrs. Cohen perished in Sobibor in July 1943.)

The widow thought it unwise for me to stay inside her house because the Germans would probably be searching for me. I decided to hide in some bushes behind the house. During the cold, windy night, I could not sleep as I worried about where to hide from the Nazis. I knew I had to get out of the Jewish Quarter, which was heavily guarded, and somehow contact the underground organization that had arranged hiding places for my sister and the other children of the Loosdrecht Youth Aliyah camp.

Av (right) in front of the entrance to the Jewish Theater, 2005

CHAPTER 5

LOOSDRECHT

On February 26, 1939, my parents initiated another emigration request. This time they were successful and received visas to travel to China, although they intended to travel illegally to Palestine instead (see Appendix C for related documents). In August 1939, several weeks before the start of World War II, my parents fled Vienna with a number of other courageous people on a dangerous voyage down the Danube River. They traveled through Hungary, Romania, the Black Sea and the Mediterranean Sea, and after several weeks arrived in Palestine. Although the British colonial powers severely restricted the immigration of Jews to Palestine, my parents, who arrived without any visas, were permitted to settle in Tel Aviv. They notified my aunt Anni Bachrach that they had arrived safely and would try to get visas for my sister and me to join them at a later date.

Based on this information, Thea left the refugee camp in Gouda for the Youth Aliyah camp in Loosdrecht in October 1939. This camp was established the previous month under the direction of Jacob and Esther Zurawel, who had come from a kibbutz in Palestine. Their goal was to teach Jewish refugee youngsters from Germany and Austria farm work and other skills as prospective pioneers in Palestine. The camp was home to about 50 boys and girls, ranging in age from 15 to 18.

When the Germans invaded the Netherlands, the couple, who had British passports, escaped to England. Joachim (Shushu) Simon and Menachem Pinkof, both intelligent and idealistic men, became the leaders of the camp. Many of the children went to work daily with local farmers, including a Jewish plantation owner, Barend Waterman, whose wife, Henriette, had a strong interest in Zionism. Their older children, Mirjam and Chaja (Ellie), organized many cultural activities for the children of the camp. The Watermans' younger children attended Werkplaats

From left to right are the leaders of the camp, 1940: Mr. Floor, Jacob Zurawel, Leo Schwarzschild, Esther Zurawel, Chana de Leeuw and Lodi Cohen

Kindergemeenschap (Children's Community Workplace) in Bilthoven. Considered one of the top schools in the country, it was led by an idealistic man named Joop Westerweel. Through their contact with this school, the Waterman family met Joop, and in 1938 he asked Mirjam Waterman to become a teacher there. In 1940 Joop moved to Rotterdam, where he became head of a Montessori school, but he continued to stay in touch with the Watermans.

In June 1941, the Nazis began deporting Jews from Amsterdam to the so-called work camps in the East. Initially, when ordered to report, few Jews attempted to defy the orders. It slowly became clear, however, that severe danger, including loss of life, awaited those deported to Poland. Accordingly, the leaders of the camp decided to find ways to hide their children among Christian families.

Menachem and Mirjam contacted various non-Jewish acquaintances for help in this endeavor. Mirjam asked Joop Westerweel to come to Loosdrecht to discuss their plans. Joop had already considered

*Loosdrecht Youth Aliyah Camp, 1941. Av's sister, Thea, is in the front row, fourth
from the left*

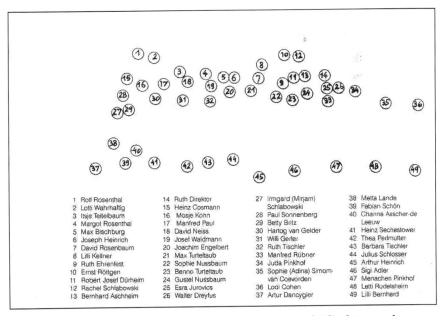

1 Rolf Rosenthal	14 Ruth Direktor	27 Irmgard (Mirjam)	38 Metta Lande
2 Lotti Wahrhaftig	15 Heinz Cosmann	Schlabowski	39 Fabian Schön
3 Itsje Teitelbaum	16 Mosje Kohn	28 Paul Sonnenberg	40 Channa Asscher-de
4 Margot Rosenthal	17 Manfred Paul	29 Betty Britz	Leeuw
5 Max Bischburg	18 David Neiss	30 Hartog van Gelder	41 Heinz Sechestower
6 Joseph Heinrich	19 Josef Waldmann	31 Willi Gerler	42 Thea Perlmutter
7 David Rosenbaum	20 Joachim Engelbert	32 Ruth Tischler	43 Barbara Tischler
8 Lilli Kellner	21 Max Turteltaub	33 Manfred Rübner	44 Julius Schlosser
9 Ruth Ehrenfest	22 Sophie Nussbaum	34 Juda Pinkhof	45 Arthur Heinrich
10 Ernst Röttgen	23 Benno Turteltaub	35 Sophie (Adina) Simom-	46 Sigi Adler
11 Robert Josef Dürheim	24 Gustel Nussbaum	van Coevorden	47 Menachen Pinkhof
12 Rachel Schlabowski	25 Esra Jurovics	36 Lodi Cohen	48 Letti Rudelsheim
13 Bernhard Aschheim	26 Walter Dreyfus	37 Artur Dancygier	49 Lilli Bernhard

Names and positions of the people in the Loosdrecht Youth Aliyah Camp photo

organizing a group for this purpose, and after the meeting, he, together with two other teachers of his school, Jan Smit and Bouke Koning, created an underground organization, later known as the Westerweel Group. The group proceeded to seek hiding places in various parts of the Netherlands. It also arranged for false Christian identity cards for Menachem and Mirjam, which enabled them to become very active in the underground.

On August 15, 1942 Erica Blueth, who worked at the Amsterdam Joodse Raad, learned that the Nazis planned to deport every member of the Loosdrecht group. She contacted Menachem, who in turn contacted Joop Westerweel. The next day all of the children in the camp, including Thea, were transferred to hiding places with Christian families, who initially had been told this would be a temporary situation. When the Nazis arrived at the camp the following morning they found the place deserted.

Thea stayed several days with a family in Hilversum and then stayed with a Christian couple near Zutphen. The names and address of the couple are unknown to me, but I know that the husband was a tailor. Thea requested that one of the members of the Hilversum family contact our family in Den Haag and ask them to go into hiding as well. Unfortunately, before our relatives in Den Haag were able to do so, they were deported to Auschwitz, where all of them were killed.

My uncle Abraham Bachrach was killed on November 24, 1943, and my aunt Anni and their children Hyman, Thea Henrietta, and Klara were gassed to death on August 27, 1943. My cousins Herbert and Renée Fink were killed on November 19, 1943. My 90-year-old great-grandmother, Feiga Feldberg, was killed on July 23, 1943 in Sobibor. Sientje Van Straten, her son, Hijman, and her daughter, Clara, were killed in Auschwitz on September 17, 1943. Joop Van Straten, Sientje's husband, was killed in Auschwitz on January 24, 1944.

My grandparents Moses and Frima Gottlieb, their daughter Peppi Fink, and her husband, Jacob Fink, fled from Vienna to Antwerp, Belgium in the spring of 1939. Peppi died in Auschwitz on September 25, 1942.

My grandparents and my uncle Jacob were deported on the twentieth convoy from Mechelen detention camp, Belgium, to Auschwitz on April 19, 1943. This convoy was the only Nazi transport during World War II ambushed by resistance fighters in an attempt to rescue the deportees. Of the 1,631 Jews on the train, 118 successfully escaped, but unfortunately I have no indication that my grandparents and uncle were among those who survived.

More than 75 percent of Dutch Jews were killed by the Nazis, the largest percentage of Jews to die from any country except Poland. There were about 140,000 Jews living in the Netherlands when the country surrendered to Germany. By the end of the war, the Nazis had deported 107,000. Of these, only 5,000 survived. Of the 60,000 Jews deported to Auschwitz, only 972 survived, and of the 34,000 Jews deported to Sobibor, only two lived to return to the Netherlands. About 30,000 Jews survived by hiding, escaping to another country, or other methods.

CHAPTER 6

ESCAPE FROM AMSTERDAM

Thea did not know I had been arrested by the Nazis, but she was aware I had been transferred to Amsterdam. She asked a member of the Westerweel Group to contact me and arrange a hiding place for me. By pure luck, on the morning after my escape from the Amsterdam Jewish Theater, a woman from the group, who I believe was Ellie Waterman (although possibly her sister Mirjam), came to look for me at the Cohen house.

Since the previous year, Jews were not permitted to travel outside the Jewish Quarter of Amsterdam, and German soldiers continuously patrolled the streets along its borders. Ellie, who had a false Christian identity card, told me any Christian caught helping a Jew would be deported to a concentration camp. She therefore planned to leave the house first and I was to meet her at the local train station for additional instructions. I ripped the Yellow Star off my jacket and left about ten minutes after her.

As I approached the border of the Jewish Quarter, I saw in the distance several German soldiers walking along one of the streets. I turned into a side street and walked one block in the opposite direction of the Germans. I then proceeded undetected to the railroad station and waited on a bench on the rail-side platform.

A number of German soldiers walked by, and one officer kept looking at me as he paced back and forth in front of me. I worried he was toying with me and intended to arrest me at any moment. Suddenly, I heard the sound of an impending train. As it entered the station, the officer moved toward the front of the platform, relieving my fear. At the same time, Ellie ran over to me, gave me a train ticket and told me to enter the train and exit at the Utrecht station, where she would provide me additional travel instructions. I quickly boarded one of the cars and sat down among the other passengers. I noticed several German soldiers among them, but forced myself to appear nonchalant. I disembarked in Utrecht. Ellie, who had traveled in a different car, approached and gave me another train ticket with instructions to travel to another town, which I believe was Zutphen, several stations away.

It was already getting dark when Ellie met me at the station. She led me to a house, knocked on the door, and after a brief discussion with the elderly gentleman who resided there, told me I would stay with him overnight and she would come to get me the following morning for the next part of my trip. As I entered the house, I was greeted warmly by the man and his wife, who offered me a tasty meal. As usual at that time, for the safety of the participants in the underground, I was not told the names of these kind and courageous people.

Not long after I finished eating, we heard the sound of heavy boots pounding on the sidewalk approaching the house. I suspected that a local collaborator of the Germans must have seen a stranger enter the house and alerted the local Nazi authorities. I ran into one of the bedrooms and searched for a hiding place. I saw a woman asleep in a bed. The room had one built-in closet on each side of the bed. I entered the closet furthest from the bedroom door and hid behind some clothes hanging from a rod.

I heard the doorbell and then the stomping of boots as the German soldiers marched into the house. One of them entered the bedroom, walked to the first closet, opened and closed its door, and walked around the bed to the second closet, where I was hiding. Out of fear I felt like hiccupping and immediately choked my throat to prevent making any noise. The German opened the closet door but fortunately for me, without further examination he slammed the door shut and, cursing, left the room. Several minutes later, after the Germans departed, I left the closet, and the homeowners informed me they expected the Nazis to return soon for another search.

We briefly discussed our next move and I suggested I look for a better hiding place. In their backyard I found a large box that contained heating coal. I jumped into the box and asked them to cover me with the coal, which made breathing extremely difficult. I had barely been hidden in the coal box when the Nazis returned, and after unsuccessfully searching the house again for me, warned the couple they would return the next morning and that severe punishment awaited them if they were indeed hiding a Jew. I did not want to endanger them any further. After thanking them for their help, I left through the back door.

It was late at night as I walked behind a number of houses. Deciding that I needed help, I approached a back door and knocked. A young man opened the door and, looking at my coal-darkened face, asked what I wanted. I explained that I was Jewish and was running away from Nazis who were searching for me. Without further ado, he invited me in, and after introducing me to his wife, who held a small child in her arms, he led me to the basement and hid me behind some boxes. I asked that he keep an eye out the next morning for a young woman looking for me at a nearby house, but warned him to be careful since the Nazis also planned to return. To this day, I am overwhelmed by the unbelievable courage and humanity shown by this family. They jeopardized themselves to help a complete stranger, and I never had the opportunity to thank them for saving my life. They were some of the many Dutch Christians who risked their own lives to save Jews from extermination by the Nazis.

The following morning Ellie managed to find me and she gave me a train ticket to a nearby town. She provided me with detailed instructions to walk to my ultimate destination. I was elated when that place turned out to be the home of the tailor where my sister, Thea, was hiding. When the man heard about my adventurous trip, he headed to the other town in order to evaluate the situation. He returned after several hours and excitedly told us that many Nazis were looking for me. He said it would be better for Thea and me to go into hiding at his friend's farm in the countryside and immediately led us there.

I was subsequently told the terrible news that the Nazis, while searching for me at the house of the elderly couple, decided the woman asleep in the bed was Jewish and also hiding there. The Nazis arrested her, as well as two Jewish boys of the Loosdrecht camp who were also hiding in that town. At the time, I heard rumors that the couple were the parents of Joop Westerweel. This was confirmed years later when I read the story of the Loosdrecht Group in "De jeugdalijah van het Paviljoen Loosdrechtsche Rade 1939-1945." On Page 83 of that book there is a photo and a description of Tina Heimann, who I believe was the lady arrested by the Nazis in the Westerweel house. She was deported to Sobibor, where she was killed on March 26, 1943.

Thea and I stayed several weeks with the farmer and his family. They treated us wonderfully. During the daytime, we stayed in a small bedroom on the second floor of the farmhouse. Several times, while looking out the window, we saw German soldiers walking in the nearby fields. After a few days, we asked the farmer if we could do some helpful chores. He requested we peel potatoes. I was very bored doing this and left all this work to my poor sister. I asked our host if he had any other task for me and he agreed to show me how to milk cows. I was a city kid, and this was probably the first cow I had ever seen. When I started to milk the animal, it bucked upward with its rear legs, startling me. The farmer laughed, suggesting I instead churn the milk to create butter. I happily took his advice.

After several weeks, Jan Smit, another member of the underground, came to the farm and transferred us to a hiding place in IJmuiden, a small town east of Amsterdam near the North Sea. Two Loosdrecht boys, who I think were the brothers Max and Benno Turteltaub, joined us there. (Years later, I learned that Max was killed by the Nazis in Sobibor in July 1943 and Benno survived the war.)

CHAPTER 7

ROTTERDAM

After about two weeks, I was transferred to Rotterdam and Thea was sent to Eindhoven, where she stayed with the family of Baron Van Heekeren, an engineer for Philips Electronics. I went into temporary hiding in the home of a young couple who lived on the second floor of an apartment building. They instructed me to stay away from the windows and to crawl on all fours as much as possible so as not to be visible to the neighbors. Although the majority of the Dutch people were anti-Nazi, a small percentage were active as German collaborators and members of the NSB, the National Socialist Movement.

I soon discovered that my host was a famous Dutch chess master and I asked him to play with me. He told me he would be pleased to do so, but he recommended I first study some chess manuals. After two weeks of thoroughly studying all the literature he provided, I learned to think numerous moves ahead. I told him I was ready to take him on, and we played five matches. Although he may have let me win, I was proud to be the winner of three of them.

Soon after, I was transferred to a *pension* (guesthouse) operated by a mother and her daughter. Two other Loosdrecht boys, Manfred Rubner and another whose name I do not remember, joined me. A Jewish teacher was also hiding there. Although the Westerweel Group provided us with ration cards, we received very little food from the guesthouse owners. The food consisted primarily of two or three slices of bread a day. Manfred, known as Papa because of his maturity, recommended we chew each bite fifty times in order to minimize our hunger and maximize the benefit of the meager rations.

The teacher left the house every day for several hours to gather material for a book he intended to write about the conditions in

Rotterdam during the German occupation. At my request, he gave me an English textbook and a Dutch-English dictionary, which I studied voraciously. I soon learned the meaning of a sufficient number of English words to understand the stories in the textbook. I found it relatively easy to learn English vocabulary since many of the words had a similarity to German and Dutch. I did not realize at the time, however, that words in English—in contrast to German and Dutch—were not always pronounced phonetically. Several weeks later, I asked the teacher for a French textbook. Again, I progressed rapidly after noticing that many English words were of French and Latin origin. After a few weeks, I asked for a Spanish textbook and began studying that language as well.

Papa decided it would behoove us to create a hiding place in the guesthouse. We arranged a few pieces of furniture to hide behind if necessary. Not long thereafter, the Germans picked up the teacher on one of his outings and forced him to reveal the location of the guesthouse. Again, we were warned by the sound of the German soldiers' boots on the pavement. Papa, the other boy and I barely managed to crawl into our hiding place before the Germans stormed into the house. They briefly and, fortunately for us, not too thoroughly searched the house and left.

We immediately decided to leave the house and try to contact Joop Westerweel. We did not know his address, but we knew he was the head of a local Montessori school. We also thought it best for the three of us to split up in order to avoid being caught together.

I left the house that day in September 1943 and had not gone very far when a German soldier stopped me and asked for my identification card. Since I did not possess one, he summoned a police van and ordered me to enter the rear of the vehicle. Inside, two Dutch policemen guarded me. The German soldier entered the front of the van and sat next to the driver. I decided I had to find a way to escape.

The front of the van was separated from the rear by a partition with a small window, and the back of the van had two doors that opened outward. I knew many Dutch policemen were not Nazi sympathizers, and I was hoping the same of the two men who guarded me. They sat on a bench opposite me, talking to each other. I stood up and began moving to the rear of the van. The two policemen continued speaking to each other. I felt this was a positive sign. I proceeded to open one of the unlocked rear doors. The policemen still showed no reaction. I hoped the German in front would not look back through the window. Suddenly, the van slowed down as it turned a corner, giving me the opportunity to attempt escape.

I pushed open the doors, jumped out, and bolted in the opposite direction. I was about half a block away when I heard loud screaming, which I think was coming from the two policemen. They must have seen me escape and only sounded the alarm some time later in order to give me a chance to flee. This further deepened my conviction that I could trust the Dutch people in time of need.

I ran several blocks and then stopped a man on the street. I explained to him that I was Jewish and had just escaped from the Germans. He quickly pushed me into an alley away from the street and offered his help. I asked him to find Joop Westerweel at the local Montessori school, tell him what had happened, and request that he please come and help me. The man took me to his home and instructed me to stay there until he found Joop.

Less than an hour later, he returned with Jan Smit, who led me to the same apartment where I had previously stayed with the chess master. Jan told me the chess master had received a notice from the Germans to report to work in Germany. Instead, he had asked Joop to take him and his wife to France. His identity card was given to a young Jewish man, who went to work in Germany in his place. The apartment then became a transitional hiding place for many Jewish children. One of the older girls from Loosdrecht, Letti Rudelsheim, who had a Christian identity card, was placed in charge of this transition place.

A few weeks later, in early October 1943, Jan Smit came to the apartment and arranged for my departure to my next and final hiding place with the family of Peter and Gertrude Beijers in Grubbenvorst in the province of Limburg. Using the standard procedure, Jan gave me a train ticket from Rotterdam to Eindhoven. He met me again at the Eindhoven station and provided detailed directions to a house on the outskirts of the city.

As I neared the house, I saw a big dog in front. The dog began growling and barking as I approached the front door. I had never become familiar with dogs and was concerned it would attack me. I took a few steps back but the dog moved toward me. I had to get to the door, so I decided to go forward, which prompted the dog to retreat, growling at me all the while. I slowly continued my advance, and to my relief, the dog kept retreating.

I rang the doorbell, and a middle-aged man invited me in. I was surprised to see Thea, who rushed to me, hugged me, and explained that I was in the house of Baron Van Heekeren. The house consisted of two mobile-home trailers with a large living room built in between them. All the furniture, including folding beds, was built into the walls, giving the house a very modern impression. I stayed there overnight and left the following evening for Grubbenvorst.

On October 10, 1943, not long after I left the interim hiding place in Rotterdam, the Gestapo stormed into the apartment and arrested all present, including Letti, Papa and six other Jewish people. Those six and Papa were deported to Auschwitz and murdered there. Letti, who had a Christian identity card, was transferred to a prison in Scheveningen.

Joop and his friends initiated a plan to free Letti. Joop's wife, Willie Westerweel, contacted a man who claimed he could arrange for Letti's freedom for three thousand guilders, a substantial sum at that time. They gave him the money and he agreed to take a letter with instructions to Letti and bring her to a local railroad station. That man turned out to be collaborating with the Germans. After he brought Letti to the agreed-upon location, the Gestapo arrived and arrested Willie and another underground member named Chiel Salome. Willie and Chiel were sent to the prison camp at Vught, and Letti was transported to Westerbork and then to Auschwitz. (All three survived the war.) Joop Westerweel immediately arranged a hiding place for his four young children. He was caught several days afterward, but was able to escape.

CHAPTER 8

JOOP WESTERWEEL AND THE WESTERWEEL GROUP

Johan (Joop) Gerard Westerweel was born on January 25, 1899 in the city of Zutphen in the province of Hilderland in East Holland. Joop learned his strong religious beliefs and sense of justice from his father, the owner of a printing business. He served as a teacher in Indonesia, and in 1932 moved with his wife, Wilhelmina Dora (Willie), also a teacher, to Bilthoven. There he became head of a progressive school called Werkplaats Kindergemeenschap. Mirjam Waterman also became a teacher in this school and a friend of the Westerweels. Mirjam's parents had a farm in Loosdrecht and were very involved with the Youth Aliyah camp there. This relationship led to the involvement of Joop in the rescue of Jewish children from the Nazis. Joop left Werkplaats in 1940 and became the head of a Montessori school in Rotterdam. Two other teachers from Werkplaats, Bouke Koning and Jan Smit, were also lead members of the Westerweel Group and, at great danger to themselves, arranged for and led many children to hiding places.

In spite of his terrible anguish over the arrest of his wife, Joop continued his underground activities with great determination, including the successful transfer of a number of Loosdrecht children via Belgium and France to neutral Spain. Arrangements were then made to transfer these children to North Africa and from there to Palestine. Also involved in these transfers were Joachim Simon (Shushu), Menachem Pinkof, Jan Smit, and Bouke Koning. In January 1943, however, Shushu was picked up on the Belgian border and transferred to a German prison in Breda in the Netherlands. There he committed suicide in order to avoid providing

Joop and Willie Westerweel with two of their children, 1937

Top row: Shushu, Mirjam and Menachem, Bouke Koning
Bottom row: Jan Smit, Frans Gerritsen

the names and addresses of other Westerweel Group members. Menachem Pinkhof, who had married Mirjam Waterman, and Joop Westerweel thereafter took over much of the border transfer activities.

On March 11, 1944 it was my sister's turn to be transferred. Joop picked up Thea from the house of Baron Van Heekeren in Eindhoven and another girl, Ruth Director, from her hiding place, and they traveled together with Bouke Koning to the Belgian border. In the process of smuggling themselves over the border near the town of Budel, they were discovered and captured by the Germans. All four were transferred to the prison camp at Vught. The two girls were transported to Westerbork on March 28, 1944, and from there to Auschwitz.

Baron Van Heekeren became aware of their situation and managed to get them transferred to a factory division of Philips in the Birkenau camp next to Auschwitz. In January 1945, as the Russian army approached Auschwitz, both girls survived the infamous Death March from Auschwitz to the Baltic Sea, during which many of the thousands of Auschwitz survivors died from hunger and exhaustion.

In Vught, Joop planned his escape. Menachem, Mirjam, and Jan Smit were actively involved in this plan. Jan even managed to talk once with Joop. The Germans learned of the escape plot, however, and arranged for a double agent to participate. During the attempted escape, the Germans picked up Menachem and Mirjam and shipped them to Westerbork. Although they had false Christian identity cards, their punishment was ruled deportation to Auschwitz. With the help of people from the Amsterdam Joodse Raad, they were deported to Bergen-Belsen instead, and survived the war. Another member of the Westerweel Group, Henk Brusse, who also was involved in the escape plan and caught, died at the hands of the Germans while in prison.

The Germans executed Joop Westerweel on August 11, 1944, one month before the Allied Forces entered the southern part of the Netherlands. His wife, who was also imprisoned in Vught, saw him once in the distance. She was fortunate to survive the war. Joop and Willie were recognized by Yad Vashem as "Righteous Among the Nations" in 1964.

The Westerweel Group arranged hiding places for about 200 people. Of these, approximately 150 were smuggled across the Dutch-Belgian border, 80 managed to cross the Pyrenees into Spain, and 70 made it to Palestine during the war. The Germans killed 23 of the original 50 children in the Loosdrecht camp.

Monument in Loosdrecht for the children and their leaders killed by the Nazis

CHAPTER 9

GRUBBENVORST

Jan Smit came to the house of Baron Van Heekeren, gave me a train ticket and instructed me to get off the train in Venlo. It was a cold, dark night in October 1943 when I, a 16-year-old Jewish teenager, arrived at the railroad station at Venlo in the province of Limburg in the Netherlands. Holding a valise containing all my possessions, I anxiously surveyed the nearly empty station platform. Jan had told me a man would meet me there and take me to my next hiding place. After several minutes a tall man walked up to me, asked my name, and requested that I follow him. I was greatly relieved when I noticed he wore the clothing of a priest. That was my first view of this brave and righteous man, Pastor Henricus Vullinghs of the Parochial Church of Maria ten Hemel Opneming of Grubbenvorst.

After we left the train station, Pastor Vullinghs asked me to sit on the back of his bicycle. He quickly pedalled along Venlose Weg to Grubbenvorst, a small village about three miles from the German border, and then along Kloosterstraat to the house of Peter (Pap) and Gertrude (Mom) Beijers. During a brief discussion in the local dialect that I only partially understood, Pastor Vullinghs asked Pap Beijers if he would agree to provide a hiding place for me. Although Pap had never met a Jew before, he consented, and Pastor Vullinghs left. One cannot give enough praise to that angel of a man, Pastor Vullinghs, who, as I found out afterward, was instrumental in saving the lives of many people sought by the Nazis—Jewish and Gentile alike—yet tragically lost his life in Bergen-Belsen.

Sitting around the table in their small, dimly lit dining room, Pap and Mom Beijers, and their grown children Wilhelmina (Mientje), Sraar and Harri, observed me curiously as I shyly but hungrily ate sandwich after sandwich of the delicious dark rye bread covered with *applestroop* (apple marmalade). At that time, my weight of around 48 kilograms (106 lbs) bore witness to the fact that this was my first good meal in a long time. That also was the Beijers' first encounter with a Jew and I am still amused when thinking of the impression I must have made.

The Beijers' home on Kloosterstraat 55 was a two-story brick house. Inside, on the left, was a large room used as a butcher shop by Sjeng, another son. Toward the rear was Mientje's bedroom, next to a staircase leading to the second floor. On the right were a small kitchen and a dining area. The kitchen had a sink with a water pump since there was no running water. Mom and Pap Beijers' bedroom and another small workroom were also on the right. The second floor consisted of a large bedroom with three beds, one each for Sraar, Harri and me.

A walkway beside the house led to a small horse stable. Behind the house was a garden with a large water pump, and further back there was a sizeable barn. Behind the barn, the ground elevated steeply about five feet toward flat fields.

Since there was no running water, we washed ourselves using a water-filled bowl, and there was one waterless toilet outside. Many times I convinced one of the sons to push and pull the handle of the outside water pump as I stood, half-naked, washing underneath the rushing water during cold winter days. They joked that I was a crazy Jew because I was not afraid of the cold water showering over me.

The Beijers were a religious Catholic family. I asked for a copy of the New Testament, and after reading it thoroughly, pointed out to Pap that since Jesus said he was not changing any of the religious beliefs of the Jews of his time, any differences that now existed between the two religions must have been introduced over the centuries by both Catholics and Jews. The Beijers prayed before each meal. Pap Beijers told me that since we all believed in the same God, I should pray in my own Jewish way.

Most inhabitants of Grubbenvorst were anti-Nazi and I learned years later that 42 of the 240 families of the village were hiding Jews. They were encouraged to do so by Pastor Vullinghs, who told them if they hid a Jew they would be ensured a place in heaven. The mayor, however,

The Beijers' home (center), 2003

The Beijers family circa 1960 in front of the monastery. From left to right: Pierre, Harri, Mientje, Marie, Sraar and Sjeng. Seated: Peter and Gertrude

51

was a Nazi sympathizer appointed by the Germans. Whenever he suspected or heard that a Jew was hiding in the village, he would notify the soldiers to come and perform a search. As a result, I initially stayed mainly in my bedroom.

Days, weeks and then months passed and the Beijers and I came to know each other well. What a wonderful family they were. We came to appreciate each other as human beings, even though initially it came as a surprise to Pap Beijers that I wanted to work with him in the fields—he erroneously believed that Jews did not engage in physical labor. Yet later, Pap instructed me in the art of planting and harvesting asparagus, and of plowing with his pony. During these months, my experiences taught me more about humanity than all my subsequent university training, and showed me the goodness and strong belief in God the Beijers and other Grubbenvorsters possessed. I observed the love they demonstrated for each other, and the unbelievable bravery they displayed during times of extreme danger.

Asparagus were harvested for about six weeks in the spring. The asparagus field consisted of numerous rows of earth mounds with smooth surfaces. Every morning just after sunrise, we left the house, put on our *klompen* (wooden farmer shoes), and walked along the rows carefully looking for any cracks in the surfaces of the mounds. The cracks indicated asparagus stems were about to come up from the soil. With two fingers, we dug around the stem and cut it off near its root. These asparagus were fresh and white and could be sold at the highest price. If the asparagus were left in the sun after they broke through the soil's surface for even one day, they would turn blue and, after several days, green. I soon became an expert in growing asparagus from beginning to end.

Since I was a city boy who had never worked with, or ridden, a horse, Harri wanted me to get familiar with their Siberian pony. He asked me to mount the pony with no saddle or reins and, breaking into a loud laugh, he suddenly hit the rear of the animal, which galloped away. I desperately held onto the pony's mane, managing to stay astride as the animal slowed down and returned to Harri. After this experience, the pony and I became good friends. It always amazed me how he turned around at the end of plowing one row of the field to plow the next, without any command from me.

A number of weeks after my arrival in Grubbenvorst, Frans Gerritsen, another member of the Westerweel Group, came to the Beijers' house. He was an expert in preparing false papers and building hiding places. After examining the house, he cut an opening in the wooden floor under Pap and Mom's bed and dug a hole underneath. He arranged it so the wooden entrance to the hole could be locked from inside.

One day in May 1944 Germans pulled up to the Beijers' house, after having apparently been tipped off that a Jew was hiding there. I jumped into the hiding place under the bed just before they entered. The Germans lined up the entire family and threatened to deport them if they did not reveal the location of any hidden Jews.

Although the Beijers knew the whereabouts of numerous Jews who had found refuge with their neighbors, they all denied knowledge of any "Jude" in their house or elsewhere. Realizing they would not get any information from the family, the Germans left. Fortunately we had been warned they were in Grubbenvorst, since it was common procedure during this time for the village inhabitants to inform their neighbors of any Germans in the vicinity.

After this episode, Pap asked me if I would have done the same for him if the circumstances were reversed. All I could say was I hoped I would have shown equal courage and human decency.

During this time we often heard the noise of high-flying Allied bombers on missions to and from Germany. I was told that a year earlier a bomber had been hit by anti-aircraft fire and fell into the village near the local church, causing substantial damage. The crew of the plane managed to jump out and parachute into the village. Pastor Vullinghs and his helpers arranged for hiding places for these pilots. He also arranged for hiding places for a number of French soldiers who escaped from German prisoner-of-war camps.

During the German occupation, it was unlawful to listen to foreign radio reports, such as those on the BBC. Anybody caught listening was subject to deportation. Since there would have been no difference in my situation, I became an avid listener of the BBC reports. The rector of the nearby monastery came to me daily and I passed the latest news on to him. He in turn delivered the information to others.

We became relatively friendly, and one day I asked him a sensitive question. I told him I was well aware there were many religions—Catholicism, Protestantism, Judaism, Islam and others—and that each claimed to be the correct religion. I wanted his opinion, not as a priest but as one person to another, which is the true religion. I was taken aback when he said that each person in his own religion has the true religion. This answer further increased my respect for the courageous and highly moral people of the village, and for their priests.

In June 1944, the Allied Forces invaded Normandy, France, and soon advanced to Belgium and the Dutch province of Limburg. In September, the Allies made two divergent advances into Germany, in between which lay Grubbenvorst. On the west and north, British and American divisions, in Operation Market Garden, advanced north from Belgium into the Netherlands but were stopped by the Germans about 50 miles north of Grubbenvorst. On the east and south, American forces secured a German city about 60 miles south of Grubbenvorst.

The Germans attacked the northern Allied Forces from a bridgehead west of the Maas River near Venlo, about two miles south of Grubbenvorst. In response, the northern Allied Forces decided to attack the bridgehead from the north, which meant capturing two villages, Overloon and Venray, which were en route to Venlo and less than 15 miles northwest of Grubbenvorst.

The Battle of Overloon occurred in early October and resulted in an Allied victory, but with Overloon destroyed. The Allied forces then advanced southeast to Venray, but suffered heavy losses. About 2,500 soldiers died in and around Overloon, making it one of the bloodiest battles in the Netherlands during the war, and the only major tank battle ever fought on Dutch soil.

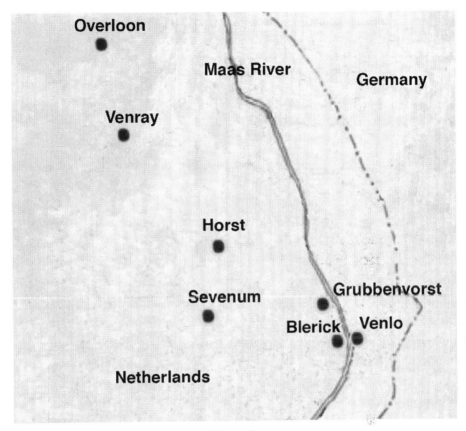

Map of the Limburg area

In the fall of 1944, as the frontline of the Allied forces steadily moved closer to Grubbenvorst, a German Army unit arrived in the village, and several soldiers were quartered in almost every house. Initially, I hid in a small area in the attic, but once the German soldiers moved into the house, I needed a hiding place outside. Pap Beijers had previously prepared a hiding place for me in the stable. He stacked straw bundles ceiling-high in part of the stable, leaving a small place behind them for me. In addition, at my suggestion, he made a small opening in the back to provide an escape route.

I immediately moved into my new hiding place. I took a long knife with me, and in answer to his question about it said I wanted the opportunity to defend myself in time of need. As usual, Pap or Mientje brought me food every evening. The stay in this location was very unpleasant and I often went out at night to the pump to wash my hands and face.

One evening, as I approached the pump, a German soldier exited the rear of the house and asked me who I was. I responded that I was a son of the Beijers. Noticing my hair was dark, and having met Harri who was blond, he became suspicious, until I told him my other brother, Sraar, also had dark hair. He calmed down and began telling me about his terrible adventures on the eastern front in Russia. I spoke with him in German, in which many of the villagers were reasonably fluent since Grubbenvorst was so close to the German border. However, I was stupid enough to suggest to him that one way to end this terrible war was to get rid of Hitler. He immediately ended the conversation and returned to the house. Afraid he would come back with a weapon, I ran into the fields and hid behind some bushes.

The next morning I approached a local farmer and asked him to let Pap Beijers know where I was. After I told Pap what happened, he informed me that the soldiers staying in his house, including the man I had spoken to, had been replaced by others earlier that morning.

Pap Beijers proceeded to build a more secure hiding place for me in the hill behind the barn. He dug a coffin-like hole about six feet long, three feet wide and two feet high. The hole was closed by a wooden cover that included a 2x2-foot opening. He also put a grass covering over the wood, and left two small openings for air.

While in this hiding place, I had to lie on my back the whole time, since the hole was not high enough for me to sit up. My only companions were red ants and occasionally a snail or a mouse. It was absolute torture lying there in the dark hour after hour. To keep my sanity, I silently calculated the increasing value of 2 to the power of x, i.e., 2, 4, 8, 16, 32, 64, 128, etc. Ultimately I managed to arrive at numbers containing more than fifteen digits. Again, Pap or Mientje brought me food and water every night when nobody was looking. I dared to leave the hole only after nightfall and could not relieve myself until then.

One evening I ventured out a little earlier than usual, just as it was getting dark, and as I walked into the field I heard people playing soccer not far away. Soccer was my favorite game, and as I headed in the direction of the sound, a soccer ball rolled toward me. As I kicked the ball to one of the players, I heard them speaking in German. Realizing they were German soldiers, I retreated to my hiding place.

Several weeks thereafter, in mid-November 1944, as I returned to my hiding place, I heard the voices of several Germans. I turned and ran into the fields, remaining there overnight. In the morning I encountered a farmer and asked him to contact Pap Beijers. When Pap arrived, he told me the Germans had found my hiding place and searched it for hidden valuables. He said it would be best for me to stay in a small hut in his field until he could come up with another plan. It so happened that on that same day, Rachel Schlabowski, one of the Loosdrecht camp girls also hiding in Grubbenvorst, had to flee from her hosts and came to hide with me for two days in the hut.

On November 22, 1944, the southern Allied forces liberated Sevenum, a village about five miles west of Grubbenvorst. The German forces continued their retreat eastward, setting up a defense line between Sevenum and Grubbenvorst. The Allies began a heavy artillery barrage against the Germans in and around Grubbenvorst. In response, the Germans left most of the houses of the village and converged on the defense line. We heard that the Germans were placing tank mines on the road connecting the two villages. All of the local inhabitants began looking for shelter from the artillery.

Rachel and I went back to our respective hosts. The entire Beijers family, including me, found shelter in the basement of their next-door-neighbor, Van Dijk. I later learned he also had provided a hiding place for a girl named Selma Aronowitz. (Selma survived the war and settled in Los Angeles, California.)

That same day, in heavy rain, the Allied Forces advanced east from Sevenum to Blerick, a village several miles south of Grubbenvorst. Blerick was strategically important because it contained a bridge across the Maas River to Venlo. The next day, the Allies advanced north from Sevenum to Horst, a village about five miles northwest of Grubbenvorst. They found Horst abandoned by the Germans.

The last bridge over the Maas River was destroyed on November 25, 1944, with the demolition of the span between Blerick and Venlo. The Allied Forces had tried to down this bridge thirteen times in order to cut the German supply lines and block a German retreat across the river. Ironically, the German troops eventually blew up the bridge as they retreated, in an attempt to stop the advancing Allied Forces. The British instead entered Venlo and other areas west of the Maas by crossing the border from inside Germany itself.

The weather improved and the Allies increased their attack, putting pressure on the Germans to retreat. In many areas as the Germans withdrew, they destroyed the villages. They had the same plan for Grubbenvorst.

Late that evening, several German soldiers came to the shelter and ordered everybody out. The soldiers intended to evacuate Grubbenvorst and bring the inhabitants across the Maas to Germany. Although we were concerned the Germans might want to use the villagers as hostages, everyone in the shelter, except for me, decided to leave and follow their directions.

Knowing it was dangerous for me to go to Germany, I decided my best chance of survival would be to stay hidden in the village and hope for liberation by the British Army, which we expected to arrive very soon. I told Pap Beijers of my decision and he and the others left. Amid the continuing noise of artillery-shell explosions, I returned to the stable and again hid behind the straw bundles. The Germans had already stolen the pony several weeks before.

After some time, the British artillery bombardment seemed to be moving closer to Grubbenvorst. The large monastery, the central landmark of the village, was hit and severely damaged. The booming explosions grew louder, and I could see flares of the fires through the cracks in the stable walls.

Deciding to leave the stable and head toward the British line, I strode to the street in front of the house. I had advanced about twenty yards when I heard a thunderous explosion behind me. I looked back and saw flames shooting up from the stable. The journals I had kept of my experiences as well as my photos were destroyed. The shell that hit the stable certainly would have killed me if I had not abandoned it moments earlier. I took this as a sign that a heavenly angel was guarding me from disaster and would protect me during the dangerous trip to the British lines.

Having heard about possible tank mines on the road to Sevenum, I proceeded carefully by crawling on my hands and knees and feeling for the mines. Thunderous artillery explosions continuously illuminated the night sky as I inched past the local monastery on the road to Sevenum. Suddenly, I heard shouts of "Halt" as several Nazi soldiers launched toward me from the side of the road. As I stood up, one of them grabbed my arm and demanded in German that I tell him who I was and where I was going.

A horrible thought flashed through my mind: *After years of dangerous escapes, so close to liberation, would this be my end?*

As I pointed to a random house in front of me, machine gun fire erupted in our direction. The British, who must have been close enough to hear the Germans, were firing at us. The German soldiers pulled me with them as they quickly retreated to their shelter on the side of the road. I managed to free myself from the soldier's grip and began running full speed back toward the monastery. As I ran, I heard the whistling of bullets flying around me, possibly shot by both the British and the Germans, and I completely ignored any thoughts about mines on the road.

The darkness of the night and my guardian angel must be credited for me not being hit by bullets or blown up by a mine. After passing the monastery, I turned left on Broekeindweg and ran to the nearby farmhouse of Pierre Beijers, another of Pap's sons. When I arrived, I was relieved to find the entire Beijers family. The British had damaged the bridge across the Maas River, and the Germans left the family to find a place to stay for the night.

Early the next morning, we saw an armored vehicle moving in our direction. We suspected it was German, and all the men immediately hid in an underground cattle latrine. The vehicle arrived at the building, and I heard somebody asking one of the Beijers women a question in English. I jumped out of the latrine and was thrilled to see two British soldiers. I asked them if Grubbenvorst was already cleared of Germans and they responded that there still were many German snipers in the village. They had barely answered my question when shots rang out in our direction. The British turned their vehicle around and moved in the direction of the shots. We ran back into the house.

It soon became quiet again, and we discussed our next move. Most of the men recommended we stay put and await further developments in the area. I told them I wanted to go to Sevenum, which had already been liberated several days earlier. After further discussions, Harri Beijers agreed to accompany me.

About an hour later, Harri and I carefully proceeded along the Broekeindweg toward the monastery. There we met another British armored vehicle. I asked the British soldiers if I could join them in their fight against the Germans. They smiled and said this was not possible. I then asked them whether it was safe to go to Sevenum and they told me that there still might be German snipers in the area. Nonetheless, Harri and I continued toward the village. On the way we hit the ground a number of times when we heard gunshots, but after a terrifying trip of about two hours, we arrived safely in Sevenum. We went to the house of the mayor, who was a friend of the Beijers. He and his wife were happy to see us, ushered us into their home, and provided us with food and shelter.

It was November 26, 1944, and I finally was

LIBERATED.

PART 2:

DETERMINED *to* PROCEED

CHAPTER 10

LIBERATED

I was ecstatic to have finally been liberated from the Nazis, from whom I had several times managed to escape the fate of death that awaited people sent to the concentration camps. Several days thereafter, the British Army cleared Grubbenvorst of any remaining German troops and advanced to the Maas River. At that time, Harri and I were pleased to have the rest of the Beijers family join us, and the mayor graciously hosted us all for a couple of weeks.

A day after my arrival in Sevenum, I contacted the local commander of the British Forces and told him I would like to participate in the fight against the German Army. He replied that he could not formally accede to this. After hearing that I spoke Dutch, German and reasonable English, however, he said I could be helpful as an interpreter with the local Dutch people, who were enlisted to rebuild the damaged bridge across the Maas River. I was elated when he provided me with an army uniform and arranged for my transportation to the bridge. There I became friendly with one of the British soldiers, who enabled me to send a letter via the army mail to my parents in Palestine.

Several weeks later I rejoined the Beijers family, who in the meantime had been permitted to return to their home in Grubbenvorst. Except for the stable, their house was undamaged. On my return, Pap Beijers asked his neighbor Van Dijk, a tailor, to make a suit for me.

Sometime in January 1945, a British Army vehicle stopped at the Beijers' house and two soldiers asked to see me. I was surprised to learn that these soldiers belonged to the Jewish Palestine Brigade; the Dutch Underground had given them my address. They came to transport me to France, from where I might be able to travel to Palestine to be reunited with my parents. I accepted their offer and with a heavy heart left my saviors—the wonderful Beijers family, who at great danger to themselves hid me from the Nazis for over a year. They had essentially become my family, but they encouraged me to go and reunite with my parents.

Years later, I notified Yad Vashem, The Holocaust Martyrs' and Heroes' Remembrance Authority of Jerusalem, of the unbelievably courageous and humane acts of Pastor Vullinghs and the Beijers family of Grubbenvorst. Yad Vashem recognized them as "Righteous Among the Nations" in 1994.

 YAD VASHEM יד ושם

The Holocaust Martyrs' and Heroes' Remembrance Authority רשות הזיכרון לשואה ולגבורה

Jerusalem, 22 December 1994

Ref: VULLENGHS, PASTOR HENRICUS - Holland (6339a)
BEIJERS, PETER & GERTRUDE - Holland (6339)

We are pleased to announce that the above persons were awarded the title of "Righteous Among the Nations," for help rendered to Jews during the period of the Holocaust.

They, or their nearest relative, are entitled to a medal and a certificate of honor, as well as having their names added on the Righteous Honor Wall at Yad Vashem.

Copies of this letter are being mailed to persons who have submitted testimonies and other interested parties. We ask for their assistance in providing us with the address of the honorees' nearest relative.

Dr. Mordecai Paldiel
Director, Dept. for the Righteous

cc:/Mr. Avraham Perlmutter, Ph.D. - U.S.A
Mr. P.J.M. Voesten - Holland
Mrs. Jutta Rosen (Levitus) - Israel
Mr. Joseph S. Landau - Israel
Mr. J.F. van den Bergh - Israel
Mr. B. Visser - Holland
Mr. Michael Lachmann - Holland
Mrs. Anne Dunkelgrun, Embassy of Israel - The Hague
Mrs. Tamarah Benima - Holland

1.5/M.P./D.W./

Recognition by Yad Vashem of Pastor Vullinghs and the Beijers family as "Righteous Among the Nations"

CHAPTER 11

FRANCE

I gathered my few belongings, including my new suit, and entered the army vehicle headed for the Belgian border. The soldiers told me that passing through the Belgian border would not be a problem, but it would be more difficult to smuggle me through the border between Belgium and France. As we neared the Belgian-French border, they instructed me to walk several miles across the fields, where they would meet me on the other side.

When I had left Grubbenvorst, I changed from my klompen to my old leather shoes. These shoes had become too small for my feet and before long I felt pain in my right foot as I proceeded into France. A few hours later I met the soldiers and continued to Paris. They took me to an orphanage, which, with the help of funds from an American Jewish group (possibly the American Jewish Joint Distribution Committee), was organized to care for children who survived the war. In the meantime, the pain in my leg became so severe that the orphanage staff arranged for me to visit a doctor. On seeing the darkened skin below my knee, he diagnosed blood poisoning and informed me that if I had come a day later he would have had to amputate my right leg below the knee. He provided me with medication and, fortunately, several days later the pain eased and my leg began to heal.

The children in the orphanage were well taken care of, and we even received a small amount of money to travel on the Paris subway. After several days, I ventured out in the company of a few other children and we visited a number of city attractions, including the Champs-Élysées, Arc de Triomphe, Louvre Museum, Notre Dame, and Seine River.

My rudimentary knowledge of French, which I studied while hiding in the Netherlands, came in handy as I traveled the Metro subway to different parts of the city. Sometimes in the morning, I purchased delicious, freshly baked French bread. Once, I even went to a nightclub and was amazed to see a number of scantily clad women twirling on the edges of a circular platform while admonishing the onlookers with the phrase *ne pas toucher* (no touching). For me the whole experience in Paris was like a time in wonderland—a complete change from darkness to light, from the misery of hiding from the Nazis in the casket-sized hole in the ground in Grubbenvorst to freedom of movement in the wide-open city of Paris.

In March 1945 I was transferred to a refugee camp in the vicinity of Toulouse in Southern France. This camp was a transitional place for children who planned to go to Palestine. I was pleased to meet with some of the other survivors, including Metta Landau and Rachel Schlabowski of the Loosdrecht camp (the Palestine pioneer camp in the Netherlands where Thea had stayed before she went into hiding). We all looked forward to traveling to Palestine where many of us had relatives. I was especially eager to reunite with my parents, who managed to leave Vienna on their dangerous, illegal trip to Palestine via the Danube River, Black Sea and Mediterranean Sea just before the start of the war in 1939.

Each day we listened to radio broadcasts about the progress of the Allied armies. We heard the news that Hitler committed suicide on April 30, 1945, and we celebrated when the German Army surrendered to the Allied Forces at General Eisenhower's headquarters in Reims, France, on May 7. We knew that Soviet troops had liberated Auschwitz on January 26, and we anxiously awaited word about whether any of our friends and relatives, including my sister, had survived this extermination camp.

In the latter part of May 1945, I was informed that my request to officially immigrate to Palestine was in process and that, in anticipation of its approval by the British Authorities, I should travel to Paris. Soon after my arrival there, I received the necessary papers and was told to travel by train to Marseille and report to a refugee camp. This trip was unusually slow because of the many stops caused by heavy military train traffic. It took about two days before we arrived in Marseille. I was taken to a refugee camp called Vieux Chapelle, and enjoyed the freedom of roaming around the city as I awaited my trip to Palestine.

Av (far left) in Paris, 1945

CHAPTER 12

PALESTINE AND THE JEWISH NATION OF ISRAEL

The name "Palestine" comes from "Philistine," an ethnic people of Aegean origin who lived on the southern coast of the Ancient Near East in the beginning of the 12th century B.C.E., but disappeared as a distinct group about 700 years later. Early mentions of the group occurred in ancient Egyptian texts that recorded a people called the *P-r-s-t* (or *Peleset*) and the Bible used the Hebrew name פלשת (*P(e)léshet*, translated Philistia in English) to denote the coastal region inhabited by the Philistines. In the 5th century B.C.E., the historian Herodotus was the first to use the Greek form *Palaistinêi*, from which the English "Palestine" is derived.

In about 1300 B.C.E., the Jews entered this land and lived under a tribal confederation. Three hundred years later, they united under a single monarch to form the Kingdom of Israel, and soon after established Jerusalem as its capital. In 586 B.C.E., however, the Babylonians defeated the Jews and destroyed Israel's First Jewish Temple in Jerusalem. Many Jews were murdered or exiled to Babylon, though some were allowed to stay. Forty-eight years later, the Persians conquered the area (then known as Judea) and allowed the exiled Jews to return. The Jews rebuilt the nation of Israel and the Second Jewish Temple.

In 70 C.E., the Roman Empire conquered ancient Israel, destroyed the Temple (the Western Wall, on Jerusalem's Temple Mount, is the only surviving wall today), killed about a million Jews, and ended Jewish political authority over the area. Many Jews fled, but thousands stayed and rebelled on for centuries, hoping to rebuild a Jewish nation. In the 2nd century C.E., the Romans changed the name of the area from Judea back to *Palaestina* to diminish Jewish identification with the land.

69

For over 3,000 years, various peoples, empires, and religions battled for Israel's ancient capital of Jerusalem. The area was successively ruled by the Jews, Assyrians, Babylonians, Persians, Greeks, Jewish Maccabees, Romans, Byzantines, Arabs, Egyptians, Crusaders, Mamluks, Ottoman Turks, British, and once again by the Jews from 1948. Of these, only the Jews set out to build a nation of their own in this land.

Throughout the millenia, a continuous Jewish presence existed in the Land of Israel, though at times their numbers were small since Jews were often treated harshly by the controlling powers, and the land was virtually uninhabitable. Despite this, the Jews always felt a deep bond with the land and prayed for a return to their biblical homeland where they could once again establish a nation. Although Jews had been the majority people in Jerusalem since the 1850s, the Zionist Movement gained new fervor in the 1880s, and Jews began to return in large numbers to Palestine. The land they found was sparsely populated, neglected, and uncultivated—a result of centuries of Turkish indifference.

The early Jewish Zionists were idealistic pioneers who intended to live peacefully with their Arab neighbors. These Jews set out to regenerate Palestine by cultivating the land and improving sanitation and healthcare, thereby upgrading the quality of life for Jewish and non-Jewish residents alike. The improved living conditions and economic advantages that resulted led to a significant increase in the Arab population during the 1920s-1940s. Arab immigration from neighboring and more remote countries (including Syria, Jordan, Egypt, and Iraq) soared substantially as they came to take advantage of the new opportunities. Although some leading Arabs believed that the Jewish Zionists were necessary to regenerate the country, most Arabs, even in the earliest days, insisted that Jewish immigration be stopped. When their demands were not met, the Arabs living in Palestine frequently turned to violence.

In November 1917, Britain issued the Balfour Declaration, which advocated the "establishment in Palestine of a national home for the Jewish people." A subsequent United Nations report indicated that "the field in which this Jewish National Home was to be established was understood at the time of the Balfour Declaration to be the whole of historic Palestine, including Transjordan," an area encompassing 45,000 square miles.

In 1920—after the defeat of the Turks in World War I, the subsequent collapse of the Ottoman Empire, and the corresponding peace conferences—the British Mandate for Palestine was established on the condition that the Balfour Declaration be implemented, thus granting international recognition for this Jewish homeland. In 1921, however, Britain created Transjordan (later Jordan) as a separate Arab protectorate out of the land east of the Jordan River, and in 1923, Britain ceded the Golan Heights to the French Mandate of Syria. As a result, the remaining area of the Palestine Mandate was only 22 percent of the original. The British also placed restrictions on Jewish purchases of the remaining land and prevented Jews from settling in the Negev Desert (the southern part of the Mandate). The inhabited part was therefore only 12 percent of the original area.

Following Israel's War of Independence in 1948, the inhabited areas were divided along ceasefire lines: 3,088 square miles or less than 7 percent of the original Mandate territory became Israel, 2,200 square miles of the remaining area within western Palestine (once part of historic Judea and Samaria) was annexed by Jordan and called the West Bank, and 139 square miles were occupied by Egypt and renamed the Gaza Strip.

Due to the insistence of the Arab countries, the British Mandatory Authority placed immigration restrictions on the Jews beginning in the 1920s. The restrictions continued in the 1930s and 1940s, despite the peril faced by Jews under Nazi rule. From 1939 until mid-1944, only 75,000 Jews (with an additional 25,000 emergency cases) were allowed to enter Palestine. Even after the war ended in 1945, the British restricted immigration to 1,500 Jews per month.

Since these quotas severely limited the option of legal immigration, the Jews of Palestine initiated the "Aliyah Bet" plan to illegally transport Jews. From 1945-1948 (the end of World War II until the establishment of Israel), the majority of Jews came to Palestine through illegal immigration. Sixty-six illegal immigration sailings were organized, but only a few penetrated the British blockade. Approximately 80,000 illegal immigrants arrived in Palestine during this period.

Because my parents were in Palestine, I was one of the fortunate few permitted to legally immigrate there. A few weeks after my arrival in Marseille, I, along with a few hundred other Holocaust survivors, boarded a British troopship, the *S.S. Mataroa*, for our voyage to Palestine. The amenities on the ship were primitive. All of the passengers, mostly teenagers, were told to sit and sleep on the crowded deck. The trip took about a week, and we were very excited when we saw the coast of Palestine. The ship entered the harbor of Haifa, and we were soon transported by truck to the transition camp of Atlit on the outskirts of the city. It was July 16, 1945, and I eagerly awaited my reunion with my parents.

Name: PERLMUTER, Adolf

BD: 18 Jahre **BP:** Vienna   **Nat:** –

List of immigrants arrived in Palestine on 16th July 1945, from France England and Italy,(left England 1.7.45) on board S.S. "Matrua".	erhalten vom WJC London
Fathers Mothers Name: Haim, Amelia	GM1
Lfd. No.: 731	Az.: F 18 – 5o Palästina

Document showing Av's transport on the S.S. Mataroa from Marseille to Palestine, July 1945
(Doc. No. 45820876#1, /Image vorhanden/_P/P0440/00465@0.1, ITS Archives)

The Atlit camp was surrounded by a six-foot high fence and we were not allowed to leave until relatives arrived and vouched for our identity. The next morning I was informed that my father was waiting for me on the other side of the fence. I dashed to the fence and was excited to see my father, Chaim Perlmutter, and my aunt Lotti Ilan. I asked my father where my mother was and he told me she was sick and could not come from their home in Tel Aviv. I was terribly disappointed and could not understand why my mother, regardless of how sick she was, would not come to meet her son whom she had not seen for six years, and who—until she received word of his survival—was believed to have been killed by the Nazis. My father told me I would be able to leave the camp the next day and travel to Tel Aviv.

The next morning, my father again arrived at the camp and I was permitted to leave with him. We took a bus to the home of my aunt Lotti on Har Hacarmel, the upper part of the city of Haifa. Upon our arrival, I was greeted warmly by my aunt and her husband, Moshe Ilan. My aunt asked me to follow her into another room, and there she told me the terrible news that my mother had died on January 28, 1945, just two weeks before my letter arrived with the news of my survival.

My mother was only 47 years old and had suffered the entire war with the terrible thought that she would never again see her children. She had obtained information about my sister's deportation to Auschwitz, but had not received any information about my situation for about two years. My mother had been treated with the newly-developed drug penicillin when she was in the hospital for a gall-bladder infection, and had suffered a fatal allergic reaction to the antibiotic.

The news of my mother's death was a devastating blow to me. I would always remember her as a wonderfully caring mother. She was very intelligent and, as I was told later, as a young woman she often sat and learned Talmud (a record of rabbinic discussions on Jewish laws, ethics, and thoughts) together with her brothers. Later in life she attended court sessions to learn the basics of the legal system. My mother had also been very active in my father's textile business in Vienna as well as in his jam factory in Tel Aviv. She is buried in the Nachlat Yitzchak Cemetery, Area 33.

The passing of my mother was a terrible tragedy for my father, especially because it occurred before he was notified of my survival. He was relieved at my safe arrival in Palestine, but at the same time we both suffered great sorrow over my mother's death and because Thea had been sent to the extermination camp Auschwitz.

After leaving my aunt Lotti in Haifa, my father and I took a bus to Tel Aviv, arriving late in the afternoon at his apartment at #8 Hamagid Street. The apartment on the second floor consisted of two bedrooms and a small kitchen, as well as a bathroom that was shared with another family on that floor. After my mother's death, my father lived in the apartment with Mr. Fink, the brother-in-law of my aunt Peppi Fink. My father and I now stayed together in one bedroom and Mr. Fink used the other one.

The next morning we walked to my father's small jam factory on Herzl Street. The factory consisted of an approximately 400-square-foot production room, a small storage room and a small office. The marmalade, made of fresh fruit, sugar and a small amount of pectin, was cooked in a large electric kettle. After a specific boiling time, the marmalade was poured into cans, which were sealed and sterilized. My father had a number of commercial clients and he personally carried and delivered the finished products to them on a daily basis. After a few days, I took over the production and assisted him with deliveries.

CHAPTER 13

THEA

Several weeks after my arrival in Palestine, we received a letter from Sweden with wonderful news from my sister, Thea. She wrote that she was among the few thousand surviving women from Auschwitz who, after a deal made between Count Bernadotte of Sweden and Himmler, were marched during the infamous Death March from Auschwitz to the Baltic Sea. She survived the forced march, during which many women died from hunger and exhaustion. The survivors were ultimately transported to Malmö, Sweden, on May 4, 1945, where they received proper care. We were elated to hear of Thea's survival and wrote that we looked forward to seeing her in Palestine.

After several months, Thea was transferred to the Netherlands, where she contacted members of the Westerweel Group, the underground organization founded by Joop Westerweel. Joop was caught by the Nazis with my sister at the Belgian border during an attempt to transfer her to France, and unfortunately was killed by the Nazis just before the end of the war. After the war ended, other members of the Westerweel Group became very active in the transfer of the surviving Jewish children to France in order to assist them in immigration to Palestine.

Thea traveled to France in late 1945 and stayed in a refugee camp near Marseille, awaiting the opportunity to illegally immigrate to Palestine (she was not able to legally immigrate due to the quota imposed by the British on Jewish immigration). In that camp, Thea was happy to meet a number of her friends from the Loosdrecht camp, who also survived the war. She became friendly with a young man, Abraham (Avram) Hirschberg, who was involved in the procurement of weapons for the Hagana, the Jewish underground organization in Palestine. Avram, an armored-car gunner in a Belgian unit of the British Army, landed in Normandy on D-Day in June

1944 and was wounded several weeks after the invasion. He had been transferred back to England for recuperation, and after his discharge in June 1945 returned to France to assist in the defense of the Jewish population of Palestine. Joining several hundred others, Thea and Avram embarked on a three-week boat trip on the Mediterranean Sea, arriving illegally in Palestine in March 1946.

My father and I were overjoyed at Thea's arrival. She and Avram were married in July of that year and moved into an apartment in Givatayim, a suburb of Tel Aviv. Thea became a kindergarten teacher and Avram began working in the diamond industry, following in the profession of his father and grandfather in his birthplace of Antwerp, Belgium.

CHAPTER 14

MARGALIT JAM FACTORY

Until his death in 1912, my paternal grandfather, Avraham Abba Perlmutter, owned a textile store in the town of Zborov, Poland. After my father married my mother in 1923, he started his own textile store in Vienna. Before leaving for Palestine in 1939, my parents decided to learn the basics of marmalade production. Soon after their arrival in Tel Aviv, they started a small jam factory in partnership with a Romanian immigrant who provided the financing. The man, who had a Ph.D. in business, was also in charge of the accounting for the company, which was named Margalit.

After my arrival in Tel Aviv, I took an active role in the company, including purchasing raw materials and production and delivery. My father's partner, who controlled the finances, allocated what he claimed was half of the profit to my father on a weekly basis. I did some basic computations of the costs of the materials, the overhead, and the sale prices of the products and concluded that the profit should be substantially more.

I asked my father to get the books from his associate, who told him he had to submit them to the tax department. This answer did not ring true. I decided to recreate the accounting using existing purchase and sales data from the previous year. The results clearly indicated a significant discrepancy from the information provided by my father's partner. My father informed him of my findings, whereupon his partner said in anger, "How dare you take the word of an uneducated youngster against that of a doctor of business."

I told my father to show the information I had prepared to Mordechai Pessel, an accountant relative of ours, for his opinion. After analyzing the data, Mr. Pessel completely agreed with my findings.

My father confronted his partner and told him that unless he agreed to terminate his association with the company, he would take legal action. This ended the partnership, and I subsequently took control of all aspects of the business. We soon purchased a motorized tri-wheeled vehicle that I used to transport the jams to our customers.

CHAPTER 15
ISRAEL WAR OF INDEPENDENCE

On the evening of November 29, 1947, I gathered with a crowd on the corner of Allenby and Ben Yehuda streets in Tel Aviv to await the decision of the UN Assembly on Resolution 181, a partition plan for Palestine. We all danced and shouted with joy when we heard that the resolution was approved and the British Mandate would be terminated no later than August 1, 1948. The United States also supported the partition resolution, but imposed an arms embargo on the region the following week.

Within days of the UN resolution, Arab irregular forces began a terror campaign against Jewish settlements. In most cases, the British forces in the country did nothing to prevent the Arab assaults, and in some cases, they even facilitated them. As a result, the defense against these attacks was provided by the Hagana, a clandestine force formed in 1920 for Jewish self-defense. The Hagana initially was composed of individual units, active in different towns and settlements throughout Palestine. Later, it grew into the central defense mechanism of the Zionist movement.

Several of our relatives were actively involved in the Hagana. A relative of my mother, Njuma Tomarkin, was the commander of a vital area between Petach Tikva and Netanya. One of the members serving under him was Ariel Sharon, who later became Prime Minister of Israel. Yitzchak Pessel, another of our relatives, was active in the organization, as was my brother-in-law, Avram Hirschberg, who procured weapons in France.

In the summer of 1947, I had approached Yitzchak Pessel and told him I wanted to join the Hagana. He arranged for the proper contact, and after some rudimentary training I was assigned, alongside two other young men, to protect an area at the border between Tel Aviv and the Arab city of Jaffa. Our weapons consisted of one submachine gun (a sten gun), one pistol, two hand grenades and a handful of bullets. We did not test the weapons, not wanting to waste any of the ammunition.

One afternoon in March 1948, several British soldiers approached the house where we were staying. We quickly hid our weapons. The soldiers entered the house, looked around and asked us whether we had any weapons. We told them we had none and they left. About twenty minutes later, a large group of Arabs arrived, armed with machine guns and rifles. Shouting, they opened fire in our direction. We hid behind a walled fence and waited until they came into range. When they were 30 yards away, we threw both hand grenades toward one of their leaders, while firing several shots with the sten gun. None of the Arabs were killed, but they stopped their advance and hastily retreated, leaving some of their weapons on the ground.

Relieved, we gathered the weapons they had thrown away in their flight. These weapons included two machine guns and several rifles. We now felt much more confident in repelling any new Arab assaults. Later we found out our experience was not unique. Fortunately for the Jewish defenders, the Arab attackers were poorly trained and disorganized; hence their assaults were mostly repelled. However during this time, hundreds of Jews and Arabs were killed.

On May 14, 1948, the British Mandate for Palestine was terminated, and the Jews issued the Declaration of Independence, reestablishing the State of Israel. Once again I gathered with a crowd on the corner of Allenby and Ben Yehuda streets in Tel Aviv to celebrate.

The conditions between the Jews and Arabs changed significantly after this date. After the British left the country, five Arab armies (Egypt, Syria, Transjordan, Lebanon and Iraq) immediately invaded. Azzam Pasha, Secretary-General of the Arab League, epitomized the invaders' intentions with his declaration: "This will be a war of annihilation. It will be a momentous massacre in history that will be talked about like the massacres of the Mongols or the Crusades."

Most countries, including the United States and the Soviet Union, immediately recognized Israel and indicted the Arabs. The United States pressed for a resolution that charged the Arabs with a breach of peace.

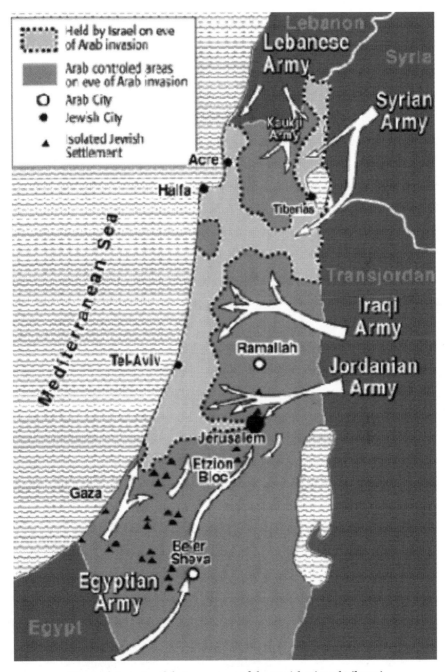

The Arab Invasion (photo courtesy of the Jewish Virtual Library)

The Soviet delegation to the United Nations criticized the Arab states for organizing the invasion and ignoring the decisions of the Security Council and General Assembly.

As sovereign states, the Arab invading forces, unlike the pre-state Jewish defense force, were able to obtain weapons through normal channels from Britain and other countries. The Arab fighters were fully equipped with the standard weapons of a regular army of the time, which included artillery, tanks, armored cars and personnel carriers. They had numerous machine guns, mortars and small arms, and full supplies of ammunition, oil, and gasoline. Egypt, Iraq, and Syria also had air forces. In addition, the British supplied training and, toward the end of the war, British RAF planes flew with Egyptian squadrons over the Israel-Egypt border.

When Israel declared its independence, however, the Jews had no cannons, tanks, or matching artillery. The Hagana had little more than a limited quantity of small arms. Only 18,900 of the Hagana's 60,000 trained fighters were fully mobilized, armed and prepared for war. Israel's air force consisted of nine obsolete planes and no warplanes. Because of the arms embargo, the Jews were forced to smuggle weapons, mostly from Czechoslovakia. Many of these had been used by the German armed forces and Nazis during World War II.

With these limited resources, Israel had to defend herself against simultaneous attacks from all directions. In the eastern and southern parts of Israel there were many isolated outposts, and the inhabitants were forced to depend on their own paltry arsenals to protect themselves. The hastily mobilized army had to take the offensive by removing the invaders from strategic positions, blocking their advance, and rushing to close gaps in Israel's defenses.

In the months following the initial attack, weapons slowly filtered in to the Israelis, and these, combined with the ingenuity and focus of the Jews, helped to turn the tide. Ultimately, the Arab war to destroy Israel failed. In 1949, Egypt, Lebanon, Jordan, and Syria signed armistice

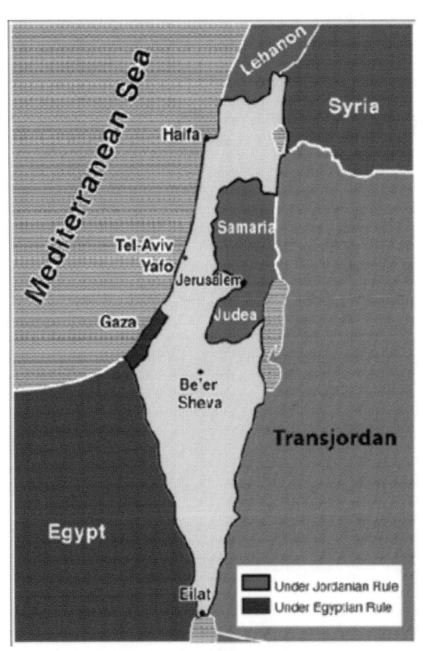

Map of Israel and her neighbors after the War of Independence (photo courtesy of the Jewish Virtual Library)

agreements with Israel. Iraq did not, and instead withdrew its troops and handed over its sector to Jordan's Arab Legion.

Victory, however, came at a high price. Nearly one percent of the 650,000 Jews in Israel were killed. Military expenditures were substantial. Many of Israel's most productive fields were gutted and mined, and the country's citrus groves—the basis of the economy of the Jewish community for decades—were mostly destroyed.

CHAPTER 16

SERVICE IN THE ISRAEL DEFENSE FORCES

On May 28, 1948, the Hagana merged with other Jewish defense groups and transformed into the official Defense Force of the State of Israel, Tsava Hagana Le'Israel (TZAHAL). Training camps were set up. I reported to the Tel Litwinsky training camp, and was assigned to the Military Police and sent to a training camp near Haifa. In addition to weapons training, we were also trained to overcome obstacles, with maneuvers such as descending by rope from a three-story building.

Our unit was involved in a number of military operations in different parts of the country. In one operation, I participated in the opening of a critical new road—the "Burma Road"—between Tel Aviv and Jerusalem. After Israel declared its independence, the Arab Legion—the best-equipped, best-trained Arab army of those invading Israel—captured the ancient Jewish Quarter of Jerusalem (in the eastern part of the city) from the outnumbered and outgunned Jews. Although the Jews successfully defended the western part of the city, it remained under military siege, and the inhabitants faced hunger, thirst, and lack of weapons. The Israelis could not use the road from the coastal plain to Jerusalem to provide supplies since the Arab Legion also occupied the Latrun fortress, located on a strategic hilltop overlooking this route.

After the Jews made several unsuccessful attempts to capture the fortress and thereby gain control of this road, Colonel David Marcus, an American member of Machal (Volunteers from Outside Israel) helped discover a winding, narrow path through the mountains around Jerusalem that bypassed the main road. Under his command, the path was quickly widened and the siege relieved, just days before the first ceasefire went into effect. Our unit investigated the feasibility of this path, and when we managed to reach Jerusalem, we were assigned to patrol the road to ensure the safe passage of supplies from Tel Aviv.

Av is shown bent down on his knees, 1948

Av, 1948

In another operation, we participated in the surrounding of an Egyptian unit headed by Gamal Abdel Nasser (who later became president of Egypt), during which he was wounded in the shoulder by a sniper. He and his men were trapped for several months near the war's end in the so-called "Faluja pocket." When a ceasefire was reached, he was allowed to return to Egypt.

Later our unit was based in a police station near Netanya. One of my tasks was to patrol the roads on my Indian motorcycle.

Av on his Indian motorcycle

On one such occasion, on June 10, 1949, I was following a suspicious-looking truck on the two-lane road from Petach Tikva to Netanya. I decided to stop it for an inspection. As I passed the vehicle at approximately 40 miles per hour, the driver suddenly swerved to the left, while at the same time a truck approached from the other direction. I instantly swerved further left and off the road in order to avoid the oncoming truck. However, the driver of that truck, trying to avoid me, swerved to his right and also went off the road. As a result I collided head-on with the truck.

Two days later I awoke from my unconscious state in the Tel Hashomer military hospital and was told I was very fortunate to have survived the collision, which occurred at a combined speed exceeding 60 miles per hour. My motorcycle was completely demolished and I was thrown back about 15 feet. My helmet was partially crushed, the skin of my forehead ripped open, my right wrist broken and my left knee damaged.

After hearing of my accident, my father, sister and brother-in-law came to visit me at the hospital and were relieved to find me alive. Several weeks later, the hospital released me, and on November 8, 1949, I was discharged from the military as a "Wounded War Veteran."

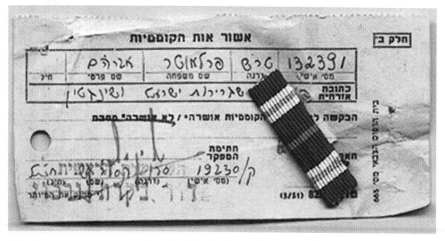

This document was presented to Av with the decoration to certify his participation in the service of the Israeli Army during the 1948 War of Independence

מפקדת הסיבה 8
‏/604
אוגוסט 1950

ב.ד.א/1
יחידה בחזקה
פרלמוטר אברהם, ת"א,צ'לנוב 65

שחרור שרות מלואים.-
הנדון: מ/13239 ס.ד.ר. פרלמוטר אברהם.

1. הנ"ל שתייך כרגע ליחידת החזקה חי"ר.

2. הוא פנה הנה ומסר כדלקמן:
א. התגייס 11.4.48
ב. ביום 10.6.49 נמצע בעת מלוי תפקיד.
ג. ביום 8.11.49 שוחרר כהצבא(מר/8/א-8095).
ד. בתאריך 8.11.49 פורסם סוב בריצות ג,
עבורו (מר/8/645).
ה. בתאריך 12.2.50 פורסם מר/8/50/137 אישור
אחוז נכות 10%.פורסמה הוראה לשחרר שרות מלואים.
ו. ביום 21.6.50 קבעה ועדה רפואית/של מטרד
כטחון אחוז נכות ל-20%.

3. אבקשך הוראתך בנדון.

ס. קצנלנבוגן, רב סרן
קצין אכלוסות

סק/סם

This Hebrew document from the Israeli military lists the date of Av's induction into the army on April 11, 1948; the date of his being wounded while on duty on June 10, 1949; his discharge on November 8, 1949; and his disability at 20%

CHAPTER 17

BACK TO EDUCATION

Several weeks after my release from the hospital, I felt sufficiently well to return to work in my father's jam factory. There was a severe shortage of supplies, however, which hampered the progress of the company. With spare time on my hands, I began investigating other opportunities for my future. I had always been interested in airplanes and now read enthusiastically about the work of the engineers who were creating new advances as a result of the use of jet engines. I dreamed of becoming one of those engineers.

A couple of years earlier, I had done some research on this subject and learned that to become an engineer one had to study in a university. I checked with the Technical Institute of Haifa and was informed that to be accepted, one had to have a high school degree or equivalent. My education had ended after the sixth grade; hence I investigated other options. I learned the University of London offered a written entrance examination, and that passing would make me eligible for acceptance not only for that university, but others as well. I decided to pursue this option.

The exam required knowledge in a number of subjects, including mathematics, mechanics, English, religious knowledge, and an additional foreign language, which in my case was German. I purchased the appropriate books, and after six months of study with the help of a relative who was a teacher, I was ready to take the tests. I was elated when I passed.

Next I searched for information about universities offering aeronautics courses. I came to the conclusion that the best universities offering that subject were in the United States. I visited the American consulate in Tel Aviv, obtained information about a number of schools in the U.S., and applied to them. Several sent acceptance notifications, and after some evaluation I decided to enroll at the Georgia Institute of Technology, Department of Aeronautics, for their Spring Quarter of 1951.

My decision to study in the United States was a difficult one. My brother-in-law, Avram, who had difficulty making a living in Israel in his trade as a diamond polisher, had already left for Antwerp, Belgium, and Thea was in the process of joining him. As a result, my departure meant my father would again be left alone, with his children far away. Nevertheless, my father urged me to proceed with my decision to continue my education, and provided me with the necessary funds for my first year of study.

Av and Thea before he left for the U.S., March 1951

PART 3:

DETERMINED *to* SUCCEED

CHAPTER 18

TRIP TO THE NEW WORLD

The acquisition of knowledge has always been an important characteristic of our family history. By age four, I could read German, Yiddish, and Hebrew, and during my four years of school in Vienna and two years of school in the Netherlands, I eagerly absorbed the lectures in the various subjects offered. During my years in hiding, I advanced my knowledge of English, French, and Spanish, and enjoyed reading whatever books I managed to obtain. I was especially excited when the opportunity arose to further my education at the Georgia Institute of Technology, one of the best technical universities in the United States. Fortunately, despite my lack of a high school education, they accepted my University of London Matriculation Certificate and I eagerly prepared for my trip to the U.S.

After arranging all the necessary travel papers, I said an emotional goodbye to my father and sister, and on March 6, 1951, took a train to Lod Airport, where I was met by Judy, my brother-in-law Avram's sister. Judy worked for Sabena Air Lines and she accompanied me to the airplane.

Looking down as the plane passed over the coast near Tel Aviv, I vividly remembered my emotion on first seeing the coast six years earlier when I arrived in Palestine. Tears welled up in my eyes as I observed my beloved homeland slowly disappearing from my view, but I knew my absence would only be for a few years.

Several hours after departure we landed in Antwerp, where Avram met me. He showed me the diamond district on the Pelikaanstraat. Later we went to eat in a fine restaurant and I was astounded by the low price of the meal. On the way back to his apartment we were stopped by a policeman, who must have been suspicious of us based on the way we were dressed.

Av and Judy at Lod Airport, March 6, 1951

Av (left) and Avram in Antwerp, March 6, 1951

The next day I continued my trip, and after a refueling stop in Ireland arrived safely in New York. I was met by my grandfather's brother, Iro Gottlieb, and his wife, Rose, who lived there. I also met with my uncle Iro Gottlieb (my mother's brother), my aunt Berta Gottlieb and my cousin Hanni. It was an emotional meeting because this was the first time I had seen them in a decade, since we had all lived in Den Haag. They also left Vienna for the Netherlands in 1939 and stayed with my aunt Anni Bachrach in Den Haag until 1941, when they went into hiding. Hanni was hidden separately from her parents in the northern part of the Netherlands but they reunited after the war and immigrated to the United States. Unfortunately, my aunt Anni and her family, who believed they were safe because they were Dutch citizens, did not go into hiding and were transported by the Nazis to Auschwitz where they were murdered.

While in New York, I also visited some tourist sites, including Rockefeller Center. Two days later, I traveled by plane to Atlanta.

Av en route to Atlanta

CHAPTER 19

GEORGIA INSTITUTE OF TECHNOLOGY

On arrival in Atlanta, I took a taxi to Georgia Tech. I went to the registration office, which assigned me a dormitory room with another boy from Israel, Gideon Nahari, who introduced me to two other Israelis, Amnon Sitchin and Tom Feuchtwang. Amnon and Tom had started the year before, and they introduced Gideon and me to some of their local friends. They had a car and we went touring with them.

Gideon, Amnon and Av (right) in front of the Georgia Tech dormitory

Gideon and Av (front) in Virginia, 1951

Amnon and Av (front) in Virginia, 1951

I greatly enjoyed the mathematics, physics, aerodynamics and English courses, and received top grades in all of them. Some of the other students often came to me for help. I received a number of high-achievement awards and was inducted into the honor societies of Phi Kappa Phi and Tau Beta Pi. I also joined the Georgia Tech soccer team as their center forward.

My friends and I became very friendly with our mathematics professor, Dr. Perlin, who often invited us to his home for a fantastic meal cooked by his lovely wife. In addition to Dr. Perlin, I also became friendly with our English teacher and often went to dinner with him. He was especially pleased when, one day while we were discussing a Shakespearean play, he asked a question about a specific subject and I answered by referring him to the exact page number and line in the book it referenced.

I also enjoyed associating with the other students. One day, a student invited me to join him and a group of other students for a weekend retreat on an island off the coast of Georgia. Not long after we arrived at a luxurious villa on the island, we convened in the living room and the discussion turned to religion. It soon became clear that I was invited for the purpose of inducing me to convert to their specific branch of Christianity. Because of my detailed knowledge of the New Testament, which I studied while in hiding with a Catholic family, I quickly pointed out to the others that Jesus was born and raised as a Jew and that, as described in Chapter 5 of St. Matthew, he said the following:

17. Think not that I am come to destroy the law, or the prophets: I am not come to destroy, but to fulfill.
18. For verily I say unto you, "Till heaven and earth pass, one jot or one title shall in no wise pass from the law, till all be fulfilled."

Av (right) and his friends relaxing in the living room of Dr. Perlin after a wonderful home-cooked meal

Av, 1951

I explained to the student missionaries that Jesus was against any changes to the Jewish laws in existence in his time, and hence I would be happy to tell them which Jewish laws they should adhere to as true followers of Jesus. The response of my cohorts was utter silence. There was no more discussion about religion, and instead of staying the entire weekend, they decided to take me back to Atlanta the next day.

I was very disturbed by the discrimination of the local white people against African Americans. One day, while taking a bus to downtown Atlanta, I decided to sit in the back of the bus, which was reserved for African Americans. When I refused the order of the bus driver to sit in the front, he stopped the bus and forced me out.

I knew my father would not be able to provide the necessary funds for my education after the first year, and therefore investigated various opportunities to make money. I began tutoring several children in basic mathematics, and their parents were pleased to see the dramatic increase in their grades.

During the six-week school summer holiday in 1952, Gideon and I went to the Catskills in Upstate New York and worked for the Brookside Hotel in Loch Sheldrake. Gideon worked as a waiter and I as a bellhop. The two-story hotel did not have an elevator, and while carrying the guests' heavy bags upstairs I always wondered why they brought so many pieces of luggage for a stay of a few days. When the tips offered to me were less than a dollar bill, I told the guests I had holes in my pockets and hence I had to decline any coins they gave. The guests generally took the hint and offered me dollar tips. I also made extra money by steering guests to a local taxi company and by bringing other guests to the card tables. Our combined earnings during the summer were sufficient to pay for most of our tuition, as well as for a used car that Gideon and I bought. We enjoyed our experience in the Catskills, and returned to work at the same hotel the following summer.

I accelerated my studies by taking extra classes during each quarter and was awarded my Bachelor of Aeronautical Engineering with Highest Honors in June 1954, after three years of studies. The more knowledge I acquired, the more I realized the limits of my knowledge. I compared this to a circle, where the acquired knowledge was within the circle and the knowledge yet to be learned was represented by its circumference. An increase of the diameter of the circle, indicating an increase of knowledge, also results in an increase of the circumference of the circle, which is indicative of the size of the unknown.

Av (right) and Gideon with their used car

CHAPTER 20

PRINCETON UNIVERSITY

During my last year at Georgia Tech, I took classes in helicopter engineering and decided this was the field I wanted to study further. Accordingly, I continued my education at Princeton University, which had an excellent research program in helicopter engineering and offered me a scholarship. I was assigned a room in the graduate dormitory, with a roommate who was a graduate student in Political Sciences. I attended classes both on the main campus and at the Forrestal Research Center on Route 1, where I also did research under the direction of Professor Leonard Goland.

With financial help from my friend Gideon Nahari, I purchased a used Ford, which greatly facilitated my travel between the two campuses. I also made several trips to New York to visit relatives and always stopped at a gas station on the road, where the price for regular gas was 17.9 cents per gallon. An interesting feature of campus life was our dress code for the meals in the graduate school dining area. All students had to wear a black graduation cap and gown, and many of us arrived for breakfast wearing our pajamas under the black gown.

I met two other Israeli graduate students, one of whom mentioned it would be interesting if we could meet with Albert Einstein, who was living in Princeton. After some research, we discovered that Einstein had a secretary who often took a taxi to shop in stores in the main shopping sections of town. One day in Fall 1954, I parked near the entrance of a store where the secretary was shopping, and when she exited, I offered to give her a ride to her house. She accepted, and during the ride I mentioned I was an Israeli graduate student and that a few of my Israeli friends and I would be really grateful if she could arrange for us to meet with Einstein.

She said she would mention this to him and we should come to his home the next day.

The next afternoon, six of us went to visit Professor Einstein. We entered the house and passed through a hallway to the left into an anteroom, which was furnished very simply. After his secretary welcomed us, she called him, and he entered from a second room. Einstein looked us over while we introduced ourselves. We stood in a semicircle around him and he cracked a joke about St. Augustine, and as far as I understood, he tried to make the point that he would not give a speech.

We began talking about politics and he mentioned that American policy was not as favorable toward Israel as it had been, and that instead the U.S. was trying to appease the Arabs. He said he did not feel responsible for this, but if he were Israel's president, it would have been his responsibility to act on this matter. I asked him why he refused the offer to become president of Israel. He replied that this would not fit him because he would not be able to express his opinion freely. He added that in a democratic country it was everyone's responsibility to decide on public affairs. He laughingly mentioned the story about the past president of Israel, Dr. Chaim Weizmann, who once dropped his handkerchief, and after someone picked it up and returned it to him, Weizmann said: "Good that I have it back since this is about the only thing I can put my nose into." He was referring to the fact that in Israel the major political power is in the hands of the prime minister. One of us mentioned the gift of a pistol to Muhammad Naguib, the President of Egypt, by U.S. Secretary of State John Foster Dulles as being symbolic of the then-current U.S. foreign policy. Einstein commented with a chuckle, "A nice man, Dulles."

When we asked if he hoped to visit Israel, Einstein stated he was too frail to do so. He expressed his fondness for Israel and said he liked most of the things being done there, but not all, and made a remark about religion. Einstein looked old and feeble, and after about fifteen minutes, he shook our hands as we thanked him for letting us visit him, and we left his house.

To earn some spending money I taught Hebrew in a Jewish Sunday school in New Brunswick, New Jersey, about a half-hour by car from my dormitory. One Sunday morning in the winter of 1955, while I was driving toward New Brunswick on an icy Route 1 and stepping on the brake, my car spun around 360 degrees. I was relieved that this did not result in an accident.

Av in Princeton, 1955

CHAPTER 21
PHILADELPHIA, PENNSYLVANIA

In Spring 1956, Professor Goland informed me he was leaving Princeton University to become Vice President of Engineering at Kellett Aircraft Corporation, located near Philadelphia, Pennsylvania. I already had second thoughts about continuing my studies toward a Ph.D., because the average period to accomplish this at Princeton was about six years. I thought some practical experience in industry would be beneficial in my future career in Israel. Accordingly, I asked Professor Goland if it would be possible for me to join him at Kellett. I was pleased with his positive answer.

After receiving my Master of Science in Engineering in June 1956, I joined Kellett Aircraft. I rented an apartment in Willow Grove, Pennsylvania, and the company soon moved their plant to the same town, about ten minutes from my apartment.

Av in front of Kellett Aircraft, 1957

I became the project engineer of a number of interesting research programs, most of which were related to rotary wing aircraft. One day in 1957, the receptionist called me and said a gentleman named Juan de la Cierva was at her desk and wanted to speak to somebody about a possible job at Kellett. I was taken aback upon hearing the name, because I knew that the Juan de la Cierva who in the 1920s invented the autogiro—the first successful rotary wing aircraft—had died during the following decade.

I went down to the reception area and met a tall, handsome man in his late twenties, who upon my inquiry about his name, explained that he was the nephew of the inventor of the autogiro. We went to my office, and Juan told me more about his background. His grandfather had been the interior minister of Spain and a friend of the king of Spain in the early 1930s, but was killed during the war with the Communists that was being waged at that time. His uncle fled to England, but soon died a suspicious death. Upon the death of Juan's father, the family was headed by his grandmother, who did not support Juan's desire to continue in the footsteps of his uncle. He decided to continue his engineering studies anyway, without her blessing.

After marrying his wife, Eloisa (Isa), they moved to Cuba, where he wanted to design a modern autogiro. He received the support of Cubana Airlines, which insisted he first design a helicopter. But by the time the helicopter was ready for a flight test, Castro had taken over Cuba. Harboring a thorough dislike of communists, Juan sent his wife and children back to Spain and traveled to the United States to pursue his ambition. He explained that he had come to Kellett because this company and its forerunner, Pitcairn, were licensees of his uncle. Without further ado, I offered Juan a job. Subsequently, he sent for his wife and children and moved into a nice house not far from Kellett. Juan not only became one of my best friends, but also turned out to be one of the most brilliant engineers and inventors I have ever met.

One of the projects I directed at Kellet was the *Stability and Control Handbook for Helicopters*, funded by the U.S. Army Transportation

Research Command in Fort Eustis, Virginia. The Armed Services Technical Information Services published the book in August 1960.

In Philadelphia, I also attended several social events. On one such occasion at a synagogue, on December 29, 1957, I met a lovely young lady, Ruth Gitberg, who had recently moved to the city from her hometown of Springfield, Massachusetts. We soon fell in love and decided to get married after my planned trip to Israel during the spring of 1958.

I also decided to further my education and applied for the Ph.D. program in Mechanical Engineering at the University of Pennsylvania. I was accepted and awarded a fellowship beginning in the fall semester of 1958.

Ruth, Spring 1958　　　　　　　　　　*Av, Spring 1958*

CHAPTER 22

EUROPE AND ISRAEL 1958

In March 1958, my friend Menachem Birnbaum and I took a trip to Europe and Israel. We had a wonderful time. We first traveled to Paris, France, where I revisited some of the places I had last seen in 1945. We proceeded to Tel Aviv, Israel, where I was pleased to see my father.

Av's father, Chaim, and Av in Tel Aviv, March 1958

I was glad to see him in good health, especially because I was very concerned about the situation during the Israel-Egypt war in 1956. At that time I seriously considered returning to Israel to provide whatever help I could. Before I could make arrangements for my departure, however, the war ended after about one week with the overwhelming victory of

Israel over the Egyptian Army. I also met with other relatives, visited a number of historical sites, including the excavation of an ancient Roman site in Ashkelon, and toured the Galilee and ancient cities of Tsefat and Nazareth.

After a one-week stay in Israel, we traveled to Athens, Greece, where we visited the Acropolis. We continued to Rome, Italy, and saw the Coliseum. We also took a tour to Pompeii and the Isle of Capri. Menachem then flew back to the United States, and I flew to Antwerp, Belgium, to visit Thea and her family.

At that time, my brother-in-law, Avram, was a well-established diamond dealer and I therefore took the opportunity to have him make a beautiful diamond engagement ring for my beloved future wife, Ruth. I then returned to New York. When the customs agent saw the ring and its purchase price receipt, he insisted the price must have been much higher. I explained to him that the lower price was a consequence of my brother-in-law being a diamond merchant who personally cut the diamond for me, and hence there were no intermediates to raise the price. He finally agreed to accept as import duty whatever money I still had left. I was happy to see Ruth, who had come to meet me at the airport, and who gladly paid for my train fare back to Philadelphia. There, I made our engagement formal by putting the ring on her finger.

Not long after, we traveled to Springfield, Massachusetts, where I was pleased to meet Ruth's parents, Jacob and Sadie Gitberg, and her brother, Wallace. They were all very nice and helped with the arrangements for our upcoming wedding.

Av in Ashkelon

Thea, Avram, Michel and Jerome, March 1958

CHAPTER 23

MARRIAGE

Ruth and I were married on August 31, 1958, in Springfield, Massachusetts. Many relatives and friends attended the wedding. My aunt Berta Gottlieb came from New York; my friends Leonard Goland, his wife Virginia, as well as Menachem Birnbaum, came from Philadelphia; and my brother-in-law's uncle Mendel Hirschberg, and aunt, Batia Hirschberg, joined us from Florida.

We had a wonderful time on our honeymoon at the Nevele Hotel in the Catskills, which was geared toward honeymooners.

Ruth and Av at their wedding

Front row left to right: Menachem Birnbaum,
Tiny Weiner, Grandpa Morris Gitberg, Ruth and Av;
Back row left to right: Leonard and Virginia Goland, Sadie and Jacob Gitberg, Berta
Gottlieb, Wallace Gitberg, Batia and Mendel Hirschberg

Av and Ruth on their honeymoon, 1958

CHAPTER 24

DYNASCIENCES CORPORATION

Our honeymoon was over too quickly and soon it was back to work at Kellett, where I reduced my workweek to three days. At the same time, I attended the University of Pennsylvania and continued my education toward a Ph.D., which was awarded to me in 1960. The title of my thesis was "On the Aeroelastic Stability of Orthotropic Wings and Panels in Supersonic Flow." The thesis presented methods of evaluating the structural stability of wings and panels of aircraft and rocket ships during supersonic flight.

From 1958 to 1960, I became aware of the limitations of working for a company without having the ultimate power of decision-making. I could not obtain approval for some of the research I wanted to pursue, and I was often directed to perform tasks that were of no interest to me. The same situation also affected my friends and co-workers, Leonard Goland and Juan de la Cierva. After considering the benefits and risks, the three of us decided to start a new company, which we named Dynasciences (a combination of "aerodynamics" and "sciences"), in 1961.

Not long after the incorporation of the company, we received our first contract. Juan conceived the idea of an image motion stabilization system. This system, called the Dynalens, is suitable for mounting on a camera or other optical instruments. It compensates for motion of the optical instrument or of a vehicle on which the instrument is mounted, and provides a stabilized image by eliminating almost all of the blurred or jumpy effect of motion.

Over the next few years this device was used for a number of different applications. The Dynalens was mounted on cameras and direct-viewing day-and-night vision instruments, on television and motion picture cameras and on devices for the stabilization of the transmission and reception of laser beams. The Dynalens had day- and night-combat experience in Vietnam, and was successfully used on helicopters, tanks, boats and spaceships. It was awarded the 1969 Academy of Motion Picture Arts and Sciences Award of Merit for Outstanding Technical Achievement.

Dynasciences also developed an Electro-Static Discharger for helicopters. This device continuously combats the effect of static electricity created by the rotating blades of helicopters. The Electro-Static Discharger reduces the static interference in communication and navigation equipment, and enables the helicopter to navigate by instruments during inclement weather. It also allows military ground crews to handle under-slung cargo shock-free. The company also invented and manufactured the Vertical Aperture Stabilizer for television transmitting stations. This product adds crispness and enhancement to a TV viewer's picture.

Dynasciences went public in 1967. Two years later, it merged with the Whittaker Corporation, headquartered in Los Angeles, California. Whittaker transferred a number of its technical divisions to Dynasciences in exchange for a majority interest in the company. I became Senior Vice President of Operations and supervised all divisions of the expanded company, which employed approximately 1,200 people. As part of this transaction, my family moved from Dresher, Pennsylvania, to Los Angeles. In 1973, I retired and sold my remaining interest in Dynasciences to Whittaker.

I later became involved in a number of business ventures, including another engineering company, real estate, jewelry manufacturing, an internet shopping plaza and a gym.

Thea, Avram and their children, Michel, Jerome and Daniella, moved to Los Angeles in 1970. My father, Chaim, moved to Los Angeles in 1973. He passed away on January 1, 1983, and is buried at Mount Olive Cemetery, Area 6, New Region 4, in Jerusalem.

Dynalens

Academy Award for Dynalens, April 7, 1970
Left to right: Av and Ruth, Isa and Juan de la Cierva, Virginia and Len Goland

The Electro-Static Discharger is shown in the circle

CHAPTER 25

THE PERLMUTTER FAMILY

My lovely wife Ruth and I are pleased to have four wonderful children. Our sons are Michael Aryeh and David Ron and our twin daughters are Sharon Malka and Keren Ora.

All of our children went to Hillel Hebrew Academy in Beverly Hills, California and finished their undergraduate studies at the University of California, Los Angeles (UCLA).

Michael continued his post-graduate education and became a lawyer, a Certified Public Accountant, and a Certified Valuation Analyst. In 1996 he married Pamela Goodman, a talented businesswoman, who created the famous SAFETY BINGO game, used by numerous companies to increase personal safety in their operations. They have a son, Zachary Roth, and a daughter, Rachel Aleeza. They currently live in Agoura Hills, California.

David continued his post-graduate education, and received his law degree in addition to a gemologist certification. For a number of years he operated his jewelry manufacturing business, Arta Diamond Corporation, in Los Angeles, and thereafter a gym in San Jacinto, California. David married Wendy Feldman, an intelligent young lady of many talents, in 1991. They have a daughter, Emily Sonia, and a son, Joshua Colin. They currently live in Encino, California.

Keren earned her Bachelor of Science in Electrical Engineering from UCLA, and she and her sister, Sharon, were the only two engineering seniors, out of over 800, who had a perfect 4.0 grade average. She subsequently earned a Masters degree in Electrical Engineering, a Masters degree in Statistics, and a Ph.D. in Electrical Engineering from Stanford University. She was Chief Scientist and Head of an International Research and Development division of America Online, and has numerous patents in her name, including several for the restoration of old motion pictures for Warner Bros. She currently lives in Pacific Palisades, California.

Sharon's academic and career accomplishments are the same as those of her sister. She earned her Bachelor of Science in Electrical Engineering from UCLA, and as mentioned previously, she and her sister, Keren, were the only two engineering seniors with perfect 4.0 grade averages. She also earned a Masters degree in Electrical Engineering, a Masters degree in Statistics, and a Ph.D. in Electrical Engineering from Stanford University. Sharon was also Chief Scientist and Head of an International Research and Development division of America Online, and has numerous patents in her name, including several for the restoration of old motion pictures for Warner Bros.

Sharon married Andrew (Andy) Gavin on June 10, 2001. Andy is a brilliant, successful computer scientist, businessman, and author, who earned his Masters degree from the Massachusetts Institute of Technology and was a co-founder of the video game company Naughty Dog. Sharon and Andy have a son, Alexander Augustus. They currently live in Pacific Palisades, California.

Michael (left) at 8 ½ years old and David at 6 ½ years old

Sharon (left) and Keren at 4 years old

Av's father, Chaim; Michael; and Av at Michael's Bar Mitzvah

Rachel, Zachary, Pam and Michael, 2011

David, Emily, Josh, and Wendy at Emily's Bat Mitzvah, 2010

At Emily's Bat Mitzvah in 2010, Av celebrated his "second" Bar Mitzvah at 83 years old

Keren, 2014

Sharon, Alex, and Andy in 2013

Sharon and Andy's wedding, 2001
Back row: Wendy, David, Keren, Ruth, Pam, Michael
Front row: Andy, Sharon, Av

Sharon and Andy's wedding, 2001
Back row: Michael, Wendy, David, Av, Bernie Markowitz, Hanni Gottlieb Markowitz,
Michel Hirschberg, Thea Hirschberg, Avram Hirschberg
Front row: Pam, Sharon, Andy, Keren, Daniella Hirschberg, Ruth

Emily's Bat Mitzvah, 2010
Back row: Rachel, Pam, Michael, Andy, Av, Ruth, Emily, Josh, David
Front row: Sharon, Alex, Keren, Zachary, Wendy

EPILOGUE

REUNION

Over the past 70 years, I have made numerous trips to the Netherlands to meet with the wonderful Beijers family and the many other heroic people of Grubbenvorst. My family and the Beijers still remain close today. Many times we have hosted each other in our respective homes. In the late 1980s, Harri Beijers' son, Henk, lived with my family and me for several years when he was in the United States to study and then to teach. My daughters stayed a summer with Henk's family in Grubbenvorst while they interned at an engineering company in nearby Venlo. I am also pleased that, despite being an ocean apart, my grandchildren and Harri Beijers' grandchildren are friends who communicate with each other through social media.

In September 1994, the village held a 50th anniversary celebration of its liberation, which my family and I attended. A number of other hidden children and their families were there as well. I was pleased to deliver a speech at the village gathering to recount my experiences in Grubbenvorst and to again offer thanks to its residents. During the ceremony, the priest asked one of the survivors to deliver in the church the Kaddish (Jewish mourning prayer) in Hebrew for the people who had perished during World War II from the Grubbenvorst area (which included two Jewish hidden children, Dutch soldiers from the village, and Allied troops). In early 2005, my family and I attended the village's 60th anniversary reunion celebration.

During my visits to Grubbenvorst, I took the opportunity to again see the places where I hid during the year I lived there. It was interesting to view the attic where I hid when the Germans were quartered in the Beijers' house in November 1944, the hill where my only companions were red ants and an occasional snail or mouse, and the stable—rebuilt after the British artillery explosion—which I occasionally shared with my erstwhile companion, the Beijers' pony.

Av and Mientje Beijers (at age 93) in Grubbenvorst, Netherlands, 2005

Av pointing to his hiding place in the attic where he hid from the Germans staying in the Beijers' home in 1944 (photo taken in 1989)

Av in front of the hill in the Beijers' backyard where a hiding place was made for him in 1944 (photo taken in 1989)

I also returned to the various refugee camps where I stayed in 1939, including Wijk aan Zee, Driebergen, Amerongen and Gouda. At Amerongen, I was amazed to find the very same swing I had swung on 65 years earlier.

I visited Rotterdam and found one of the houses in which I hid. I also met again with Jan Smit. Jan had arranged hiding places for me in both Rotterdam and Grubbenvorst.

Av swinging on the same swing he enjoyed in the
refugee camp of Amerongen in 1939 (photo taken in 2005)

Ruth and Av in front of one of Av's hiding places in Rotterdam, Netherlands, 1994

Several times I traveled to Amsterdam. On one occasion, I visited the Jewish Theater, where the German soldiers had taken me after my capture in March 1943. While in the city, I also tried to find out about the Cohen family, who provided a home for me for several months. I was unsuccessful until 2005, when I contacted Mr. Hans Gewin of the Dutch city of Zutphen and asked for his assistance. Shortly after, he sent me a letter that indicated I had stayed at Muiderschans (now called Sarphati Street) 101, with the widow Cohen-Branden. The letter also provided details about her children. Using this information and my recollections, I deduced that unfortunately the Cohen son who had been picked up and taken with me to the Jewish Theater was killed in 1943 in either Auschwitz or Sobibor, and that Mrs. Cohen was killed in Sobibor that same year.

Av in front of the monument in the interior of the Jewish Theater, where only the outer walls still remain, 2005

Partial list on one of the walls of the Jewish Theater of the people deported and killed by the Nazis. Perlmutter is second from the bottom in the right column. It probably refers to somebody else with the same last name.

I returned a number of times to Israel to visit both relatives and friends. On one visit in September 1994, I was pleased to meet once more with Letti Rudelsheim (now called Aviva Ben Cheled), one of the Loosdrecht camp members, whom I had not seen since she was placed in charge of one of my hiding places in Rotterdam. I also met again with Mirjam Waterman, a prominent member of the Westerweel Group.

While in Israel, I also visited Yad Vashem, The Holocaust Martyrs' and Heroes' Remembrance Authority of Jerusalem. The experience was informative and emotional. I had previously notified the organization of the courageous and humane acts of Pastor Vullinghs and the Beijers family, and I was pleased that in 1994 Yad Vashem recognized them as "Righteous Among the Nations."

Av and Letti in Israel, 1994

With the exception of the Poles, more Dutch have been honored by Yad Vashem as "Righteous Gentiles" than citizens of any other country. Unfortunately I do not know the names and addresses of many of the other Catholic and Protestant men and women who endangered their own lives and those of their family members to hide me, a Jewish teenage stranger, from the Nazis. They are equally to be considered as "Righteous Among the Nations." Their actions demonstrated a truism that should be announced daily to all people of the world: Regardless of which religion or belief we associate ourselves with, the most important Golden Rules are

"DO UNTO OTHERS AS YOU WOULD HAVE OTHERS DO UNTO YOU"

and

"DO NOT DO UNTO OTHERS WHAT YOU DO NOT WANT OTHERS TO DO UNTO YOU"

APPENDICES

CHRONOLOGY, 1939-1945

This section provides a summary of the various places I lived once I left Vienna, Austria, on January 11, 1939—at the age of 11—until arriving in July 1945 in the future State of Israel.

January 11, 1939-December 1939: Various refugee camps in the Netherlands (Wijk aan Zee, Driebergen, Amerongen, Gouda), ending with a hospital stay at the quarantine camp Zeeburgerdijk in Amsterdam

December 1939-October 7, 1942: Den Haag (living with the Van Straten family)

October 7, 1942-March 1943: Amsterdam (living with the Cohen family)

March 1943: Caught by Nazis and brought to the Jewish Theater. Escaped from the theater and then from Amsterdam via train

March-October 1943: Various hiding places (Zutphen, IJmuiden, Rotterdam, Eindhoven); Captured in Rotterdam (in September) but subsequently escaped

October 1943-November 26, 1944: Hidden in Grubbenvorst

November 26, 1944: Liberated by British Army

November 26, 1944-December 1944: Sevenum

December 1944- January 1945: Grubbenvorst

January-March 1945: Orphanage in Paris, France

March-May 1945: Refugee camp in Toulouse, France

May 1945: Paris, France

June-July 1945: Refugee camp in Marseille, France

Locations Av stayed in from 1939-1945 in the Netherlands:

1: Wijk aan Zee	2: Driebergen
3: Amerongen	4: Gouda
5: Amsterdam	6: Den Haag (The Hague)
7: Amsterdam	8: Zutphen
9: IJmuiden	10: Rotterdam
11: Eindhoven	12: Grubbenvorst

NETHERLANDS-RELATED DOCUMENTATION

I have included a number of documents that provide information about my stay in the Netherlands.

The first page of this registration document shows the date and place of my birth and the dates of my arrival in the Netherlands (January 11, 1939) and in Amsterdam (October 7, 1942). The document indicates I arrived in Amsterdam from Scheldestraat 42 in Den Haag (where I stayed with the Van Straten family) as an evacuee from the coast. Also shown are the names of my parents, who were living in Tel Aviv, and the different cities in which I stayed. In the second-to-last column of the second page it states that I was not deported from Amsterdam.

Page 1 of registration document providing information on Av's stay in the Netherlands

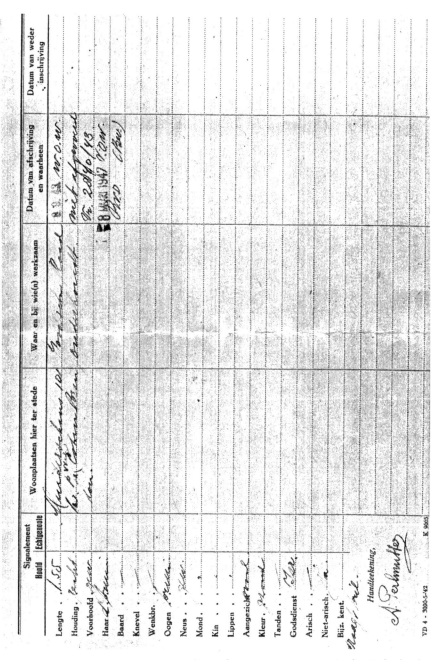

Page 2 of registration document providing information on Av's stay in the Netherlands

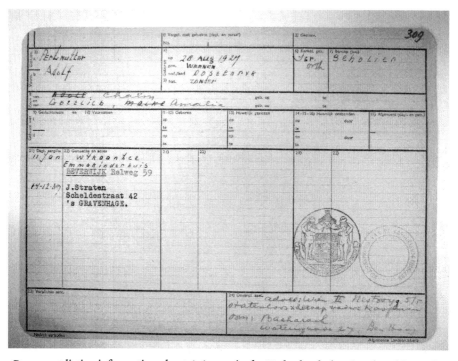

Document listing information about Av's stay in the Netherlands (National Archives, The Hague, Zorg voor de vluchtelingen uit Duitsland, 1938-1942, 2.04.58, inv. nr. 130)

JOODSCH VLUCHTELINGENKAMP
QUARANTAINE INRICHTING ZEEBURG
AMSTERDAM-O.   TEL: 50339

LIJST VAN BACILLENDRAGERS

d.d. 7 October 1939

NAAM	GEBOREN	GEKOMEN UIT
1. WEISZBARD, Fella	17-10-1929	
2. BUCH, Gisela	19-10-1924	Cromvliet
3. HARTMANN, Siegmund	3-5-1929	Soesterberg
4. DAVIDS, Werner	25-9-1928	Burger Weeshuis
5. MAYER, Friederich	29-5-1926	" "
6. PLESSNER, Wolfgang	13-4-1930	" "
7. GOLD, Hermann	17-10-1933	" "
8. LINDENBAUM, Hans	21-10-1932	" "
9. HIRSCHBERG, Rolf	1-8-1933	" "
10. EICHENWALD, Fritz	4-7-1928	" "
11. HOROWITZ, Josef	10-7-1931	" "
12. ANGRESS, Wolfgang	22-8-1924	" "
13. SCHONER, Edith	1-8-1932	Hoogstr., R'dam
14. MAYERHOF, Inge	1-7-1930	Burger Weeshuis
15. LEHMANN, Werner	21-5-1930	" "
16. EICHENWALD, Hanna	12-10-1925	" "
17. ABRAHAM, Bertram	2-3-1927	" "
18. BLUMENTHAL, Léonie,Marion	20-12-1934	Spieringstr, Gouda
19. EISNER, Erik	3-6-1925	" "
20. GOLDBACH, Helmut	29-8-1927	" "
21. GOLDSCHMIDT, Karl,Nathan	9-11-1926	" "
22. HANAUER, Heinz,Hieronymus	26-5-1925	" "
23. HECHT, Herbert, Kurt	6-3-1923	" "
24. HIRSCHBERG, Heinz, Martin	19-10-1925	" "
25. LEVY, Hans, Robert	2-2-1927	" "
26. LIEMANN, Ruth	16-2-1923	" "
27. PERLMUTTER, Adolf	28-8-1927	" "
28. RIP, Norbert	4-9-1927	" "
29. SALOMON, Hans	30-12-1926	" "
30. SCHNITZER, Moritz	4-2-1922	" "
31. STIEFEL, Kurt	20-6-1928	" "
32. LAUB, Anna	24-12-1932	" "
33. BECK, Walter	6-4-1932	Amsterdam
34. ELIANOEWITZ, Ruth	22-3-1932	Burger Weeshuis
35. ADVOKAT, Walter	13-10-1922	" "
36. METZGER, Hedy	24-12-1926	Spieringstr. Gouda
37. WINGENS, Günther	7-1-1932	Burger Weeshuis
38. BRUCH, Herbert	17-10-1932	" "
39. KWIAT, Erwin	3-4-1931	" "
40. BIEGELEISEN, Ruth	5-5-1928	" "
41. SALOMONS, Bodo	4-2-1927	" "
42. WETZLAR, Rudi	28-1-1934	" "
43. NAGEL, Eva	7-2-1928	" "
44. KATZ, Günther	1-7-1926	" "
45. HELMREICH, Josef	26-10-1927	" "
46. SCHAUMBERG, Joachim	14-1-1932	" "

JOODSCH VLUCHTELINGENKAMP
QUARANTAINE INRICHTING ZEEBURG
AMSTERDAM-O.   TEL: 50339

The list of bacilli carriers (sick children) transferred to the quarantine facility in Amsterdam. Av is listed under 27 and as coming from Gouda (National Archives, The Hague, Zorg voor de vluchtelingen uit Duitsland, 1938-1942, 2.04.58, inv. nr. 127)

APPENDIX C

1938 AND 1939 EXIT APPLICATION AND TRAVEL DOCUMENTS

Shown here are the documents provided to me by the United States Holocaust Memorial Museum in Washington, D.C. regarding the efforts of my parents, Chaim and Malka Perlmutter, to leave Vienna in May 1938.

The first five pages are questionnaires filled in by my father. He submitted these documents, in German, to the Emigration Department of the Assistance Center of the Israelite Culture Organization. On the first page, my father wrote his name, Chaim Perlmutter; address, Nestroygasse #5 Apartment 2; birthdate, May 15, 1895; birthplace, Zborov, Poland; citizenship, Polish, and that he had been living in Vienna since 1918. He also stated that his occupation was a businessman with no monthly income, that he spoke German and Polish, and that he provided registration documents to the Polish Consulate.

On the second page, he answered that he wants to emigrate to the U.S.A., Australia, Canada, Palestine or wherever there was a possibility. He wrote that his family consisted of his wife, Amalia (Malka), who was born on July 18, 1897, his schoolgirl daughter, Dorothea, and his schoolboy son, Adolf, and that he wants us all to leave together. He submitted the document on May 18, 1938. His request for emigration, however, was unsuccessful.

The following year, on February 26, 1939, he initiated another emigration request, as indicated in the third and fourth documents. This time he indicated he was without any citizenship, learned to be a bookbinder, spoke German and Hebrew and had all the necessary emigration documents. He also wrote that he wanted to immigrate to Palestine, and provided the name and address of a cousin in Haifa, Palestine.

The fifth document shows his request for travel to Palestine, also dated February 26, 1939. The subsequent document shows the confirmation by the Israelite Culture Organization that Chaim Perlmutter paid 800 of the 1200 German Marks travel cost for himself and his wife, that his children, Dorothea and Adolf, had been sent to Holland via a Kindertransport and that the information on his emigration request was believable.

The subsequent documents are receipts of the payments of 400 German Marks each for Chaim and his wife for the travel costs to China. They received visas to travel to China, although they intended to illegally travel to Palestine. The final two documents are receipts of transportation charges of 1200 German Marks each for Chaim and Malka. In August 1939, my parents traveled by boat down the Danube River from Vienna via Hungary and Romania to the Black Sea and from there illegally by boat to Palestine, where they arrived before the start of World War II.

Page 1 of the questionnaire submitted to the Emigration Department by
Av's father on May 18, 1938. This request was denied.

Page 2 of the questionnaire submitted to the Emigration
Department by Av's father on May 18, 1938. This request was denied.

*Page 1 of the questionnaire submitted to the
Emigration Department by Av's father on February 26, 1939*

Wohin wollen Sie auswandern: *Palästina*

Welche Pläne haben Sie für Ihren neuen Aufenthalt? *Arbeiten*

Welche Mittel stehen Ihnen für die Auswanderung zur Verfügung?

Welche Beziehungen haben Sie im Ausland, besonders in dem Land, wohin Sie auswandern wollen?

	Vor- und Zuname	Wohnort	Genaue Adresse	Verwandtschaftsgrad
a) Verwandte	*Moses Silber*	*Haifa*	*Rechov Gilead*	*Cousin*
b) Freunde				

Referenzen

Haben Sie einen gültigen Paß? *ja*
Ausgestellt von *Wien* gültig bis

Angehörige

Verwandtschaftsgrad	Name	Geburtsort	Geburtsdatum	Beruf
1) *Gattin*	*Malke Perlmütter*	*18/9 1897*	*18/9 1897*	*Haushalt*
2)		*Przemyśl?*		
3)				
4)				
5)				
6)				
7)				
8)				
9)				
10)				

Welche der obgenannten Angehörigen sollen jetzt und welche später auswandern?

Wien, am *26/2* 193*9*   *Chaim Perlmütter*
Unterschrift

Page 2 of the questionnaire submitted to the Emigration Department by Av's father on February 26, 1939

ISRAELITISCHE KULTUSGEMEINDE
Auswanderungsabteilung (Gruppe Abfertigung),

Wien I.

ANSUCHEN

des (der) *Chaim Perlmütter u. Frau Malka Perlmütter*

wohnhaft I. Bezirk, *Hochweg* Straße Nr. *5* Tür *5*

frühere Wohnung

um einen Beitrag an den Reisebpasen für sich und für die mitreisenden Familienmitglieder.

NAME: ADRESSE: VERWANDTSCHAFTSGRAD:

Ich (wir) beabsichtige(n) am _____ nach *Palestina*

auszuwandern. Ich bin (wir sind) im Besitze eines gültigen *Passes*

Reisepasses und eines Einreisevisums nach *Palestina*

(event. Durchreisevisum anzugeben)

Derzeit stehen mir (uns) zur Verfügung RM

in Worten:

Der seinerzeit bei der Kultusgemeinde eingereichte Registrierungsbogen trägt die Nr.

Wien, am *26/5*

Von der Partei nicht auszufüllen:

Eingelaufen am _____ Zur Recherche am

Vorgeladen für den _____ Erledigt unter W

Nur einzureichen, wenn bereits eine Einreisemöglichkeit (gültiger Reisepaß und Einreisevisum) vorhanden ist.

Request for travel to Palestine, dated February 26, 1939

Confirmation by the Israelite Culture Organization of
Av's father's claims on his questionnaire

Erfordernis.   Deckung:

Dokumente: Visa .... RM ....   Partei aufgebracht RM ....

s. ....   noch aufbringbar   . ...

Bahr }   Hilfsaktionen   . ...
        Oesterreich .
Schiff }   .   ...

Transportspesen ....   RM ....

....   Es fehlen somit   . ...

Antrag

auf Bewilligung eines Betrages von

    RM. 4 rv — (In Worten Vierhundert ....)

Wien, 26. Feb. 1939

                                    Unterschrift:

Anzahl der Personen .... fährt (fahren) mit Dampfer ....

der Schiffahrtsgesellschaft .... Type A

am .... ab Hafen: .... nach Hafen: ....

             Zielland: .... CHINA

*Receipt of payment of 400 German Marks each for
Chaim and his wife for the travel costs to China*

157

Auswanderungsabteilung
der Isr.Kultusgemeinde, Wien
I.Seitenstettengasse 6

Wien, &.. .. .. 1939. 1939.

W.No. ...110...

Titl.

Transport A

Wien.

Wir erklären uns bereit, zu den Reisekosten

der
des _____ nach CHINA

RM Hun - (in Worten) Vierhundert/

beizutragen.

Dieser Betrag kann mittels Erlagschein überwiesen oder
gegen Vorweisung dieses Schreibens u. einer Inkassobestätigung vor-
mittags in unserer Auswanderungsabteilung,Tür 16 behoben werden. In
letzterem Falle ist telefonische Anmeldung zweckmässig.

Es wird darauf aufmerksam gemacht, dass ohne ausdrück-
liche Zustimmung der Auswanderungsabteilung der Isr.Kultusgemeinde,
Wien,weder die vorgeschriebene Reiseroute geändert, noch ein Geldbetrag
zu Handen der Partei rückerstattet werden darf.

Hochachtungsvoll
AUSWANDERUNGSABTEILUNG
der israelischen Kultusgemeinde

Receipt of payment of 400 German Marks each for Chaim and his wife for the travel costs to China

Receipts of transportation charges of 1200 German Marks for Av's father, Chaim

Receipts of transportation charges of 1200 German Marks for Av's mother, Malka

BIBLIOGRAPHY

Bard, Mitchell G. "History." Jewish Virtual Library, http://www.jewishvirtuallibrary.org/jsource/History/history.html

Brasz, Ineke and M. Pinkhof. "De jeugdalijah van het Paviljoen Loosdrechtsche Rade 1939-1945." Second Printing. Hilversum: Historische Kring Loosdrecht – Verloren, 1998.

"The Central Database of Shoah Victims' Names." Yad Vashem, http://db.yadvashem.org/names/search.html?language=en

"Digital Monument to the Jewish Community in the Netherlands." Jewish Historical Museum, http://www.joodsmonument.nl/

Habas, Bracha. *His Inner Light, The Life and Death of Joop Westerweel.* Bnei Brak: Publishing House of Kibbutz Hameuchad, Ltd. (published in Hebrew), 1964.

Keesing, Miriam. "Welcome to DOKIN." dokin, http://dokin.nl

Schreiber, Marion. *The Twentieth Train: The True Story of the Ambush of the Death Train to Auschwitz.* New York: Grove Press, 2005.

Woolf, Linda. "Survival and Resistance: The Netherlands Under Nazi Occupation." Paper presented at the United States Holocaust Memorial Museum, April 6, 1999, http://www2.webster.edu/~woolflm/netherlands.html

To view Av's 1997 interview for Steven Spielberg's Shoah Visual History Foundation: https://www.youtube.com/watch?v=PfvMp3N7tbs

ABOUT THE AUTHOR

Avraham Perlmutter was born in Vienna, Austria, in 1927. A Holocaust survivor, he emerged with a positive perspective on life—choosing to focus on the people who helped him rather than those set on defeating him. After World War II, he fought in the Israeli War of Independence to help establish the State of Israel. He went on to pursue his education in the United States, earning a Ph.D. in aeronautical engineering. Fluent in seven languages, he is an award-winning scientist and a successful businessman.

Avraham currently lives in Santa Monica, California, with his wife, Ruth. Together they have four children and five grandchildren. He continues to share his story with community groups and schools and through his Shoah Foundation interview—hoping to inspire people to help others in need, achieve an education, and overcome difficulties in pursuit of their dreams.

Made in the USA
Middletown, DE
02 September 2021

47504191R00104